UNDERSTANDING
WOODCARVING
in the ROUND

The best from **WOODCARVING** *magazine*

UNDERSTANDING WOODCARVING in the ROUND

The best from **WOODCARVING** *magazine*

GUILD OF MASTER CRAFTSMAN PUBLICATIONS LTD

This collection first published 1998
by Guild of Master Craftsman Publications Ltd,
Castle Place, 166 High Street, Lewes, East Sussex BN7 1XU

Reprinted 1998

Printed and bound by Kyodo Printing (Singapore) under the supervision of
MRM Graphics, Winslow, Buckinghamshire, UK

Front cover photographs supplied by Andrew Thomas

CONTENTS

NOTES

PLEASE NOTE that names, addresses, prices etc. were correct at the time the articles were originally published, but may since have changed.

MEASUREMENTS

THROUGHOUT the book instances will be found where a metric measurement has fractionally varying imperial equivalents, usually within $\frac{1}{16}$ in either way. This is because in each particular case the closest imperial equivalent has been given. A mixture of metric and imperial measurements should NEVER be used – always use either one or the other.

INTRODUCTION

THERE is no doubt that interest in woodcarving, whether for pleasure or for profit, is undergoing a revival. Sated with soulless electronic technology and bland mass production, people are rediscovering the pleasures of making things for themselves with their own hands, and of carving natural materials like wood.

With this renaissance in crafts in general, and woodwork in particular, has come an increase in demand for learning the old skills and techniques which were once taught in schools or handed down through apprenticeships.

In this book of articles selected from *Woodcarving* magazine you will find not only detailed how-to project articles but also features on skilled woodcarvers both amateur and professional who will inspire you to emulate their expertise.

This book concentrates on carving in the round, and the 20 projects include animals – from birds, whales and horses to rats, lizards and fish – as well as human figures and ecclesiastical works. There is even an article on copy-carving.

The 10 features look at the work of top carvers such as Terry Warren, Paul Kedwards, Colin Hickman and Ernest Muehlmatt.

If you enjoy carving animals or figures in the round there is bound to be something in this book to both instruct and inspire you.

Nick Hough
Editor, *Woodcarving*

"He has a good sense of finish" remarked my old primary school teacher with reference to a three-pronged candle holder I had made as a 10-year-old. The edges were not just bevelled, but sanded round and smooth. Even now I sometimes think the things I make are just an excuse to make a piece of wood smooth.

I also remember vividly the pleasure of peeling bark from a hazel arrow or bow with a sharp penknife. How lucky to be able to earn money from the similar sensation of a gouge slicing through lime.

I am not particularly interested in technical virtuosity or pieces which have a deep meaning or story behind them. I acknowledge the limitations of my skill and my need for a steady stream of sales.

So my work is shaped by these constraints, and my untutored eye for simple shapes, composition, contrasts of colour, materials and the all important finish.

My sculptures fall into three main categories. First a range of stylised designs carved in lime (*Tilia vulgaris*) and stained with Liberon pastel shade wood dyes.

The pieces in *Bread and Butter* were bandsawn from two profiles, before I made free cuts with the bandsaw from all angles to remove as much stock as possible.

I could use grinders, Kutzalls and so on to achieve the rough shape of these simple forms, but I actually enjoy using gouges and it is good to spend some time dust free.

I have only nine carving tools: four gouges, two skew chisels, two spoon gouges and a small V tool, and it is still amazing how frequently I cannot find the one I need.

Flap wheels (80 grit) do most of the sanding, followed by 120, then 220 grit wet and dry paper. English Abrasives wet and dry has just the right degree of flexibility and stiffness to create curves and folds which enable fine shaping as well as finishing, but I do not sand any finer because the stain is less well absorbed into a truly smooth finish.

Expressing essence

I am looking for simplicity of shape and form, to produce completely assured, confident pieces of work. When sculpting you are well aware when you are bluffing or fudging, when your lack of complete knowledge of the subject causes you to hesitate. Often, this is the space between details.

You may understand the beak and the eye separately, but the space where they merge into one another is less tangible, but equally important.

In a similar way a cartoonist or computer wizard can exaggerate features without losing the essence of a subject. There can be many right solutions to the problem of finding the essence of the subject, without merely creating an anatomically correct model.

The sculptor Brancusi commented, "What is real is not the external form, but the essence of things. It is impossible to express anything essentially real by imitating its exterior."

Main picture **Bread and Butter.**
Right **Kingfisher** 200mm, 8in high.
Far right **Flint** 330mm, 13in high.

SMOOTH

Composite carvings

The second type of sculpture I do tends to be a smaller, more detailed carving of a lizard, snail, bird or fish. This is married to weathered yew (*Taxus baccata*) or oak (*Quercus robur*), which is in turn mounted on burr elm (*Ulmus spp*) or spalted beech (*Fagus spp*).

The *Kingfisher* in yew is typical of this approach. The bird was screwed to a block of wood for rough carving, and these holes were later the mounting points for screws which were set in Araldite to the base.

I took the sanding to 600 grit, into which I freshly carved details to the throat and cheeks.

In this case the immediate base was a piece of weathered yew root, wire brushed, scoured with oven cleaner and dipped in Cuprinol 5 star wood treatment.

It was angled to emphasise and compliment the pose of the bird and mounted on a base of spalted beech. The black spalting suggested ripples through the blue-green stain.

This was a deliberate composition of colour and materials to produce a sculpture that could be viewed with satisfaction from many angles.

Spontaneous sculpture

The last and most enjoyable type of sculpture is more individual and tends to grow from ideas conceived while working on my bread and butter styles.

The *Flint* came from work on a stained golden plover, where I made cuts with a scalpel blade to stop black stain running with the grain. When it was washed over with white stain, and the surplus was wiped clear, there was an abrupt change from black to white which echoed the contrast from chalky outer, to steely black silica inside a real flint.

My *Flint* was made from spalted lime which was great fun to make and provided plenty of opportunity to experiment with stains and pure shape. But how to sell a flint?

FEATURE In his sculptures Terry Warren concentrates on the finish and essence of his subjects

& SIMPLE

Two Trout
550mm, 21⅝in.

Man With Birds
470mm, 18⅜in high.

Flowing ideas

The *Two Trout* in lacewood (*Platanus hybrida*) were inspired by a Tunnicliffe print in which a kingfisher sits, looking down on a host of salmon weaving their way against the flow of a stream.

The base, which was carved in elm, was the enjoyable part, my intention being to suggest water surging over smoothed rocks.

With a rotary wire brush in a power drill I ripped out the soft grain and stained it with overlays of blue-green, black spirit and water stains.

From certain angles it was possible to interpret the base as a whale's belly, the wire brushed effect mimicking a Baleen whale's throat grooves. This led me on to the *Whale's Head* project.

Because of the larger scale, the grooves on the *Whale's Head* had to be wider and deeper than the wire brushed technique could achieve, so I carved them with gouge and skew.

A suggestion of an eye extending from the throat grooves, blow-hole and slightly pronounced lips completed a fairly simple carving. The key to this sculpture was the angle of the head being tilted both forwards and sideways.

I coloured the underbelly with white and blueberry stain, and the whole carving was overlain with black, strategically wiped back to reveal grain and colour.

As with all my pieces, I sealed the wood with diluted polyurethane varnish, re-sanded and waxed with Craft Supplies paste wax, before polishing with a rotary brush held in the chuck of an electric motor.

As a forager for, and collector of wood suitable for bases, the idea of developing sculpture from found materials is one I am keen to pursue.

Whale's Head,
350mm, 14in high.
Bird With The Wind In His Hair, 380mm, 15in.

Birdman

The Bird With Wind In His Hair was assembled from yew root, flint and honeysuckle vine (*Lonicera spp.*), with the body featuring a section of yew root which had grown round and enveloped a large flint.

I think it would be difficult to be too premeditated about this technique, but it is useful to have a floating idea at the back of the mind, to take advantage of unusual materials as they come to hand.

Many of my carvings feature birds because they are so accessible and evoke many different meanings for people. Chirpy sparrows, graceful sea-birds, and elegant doves are just a few.

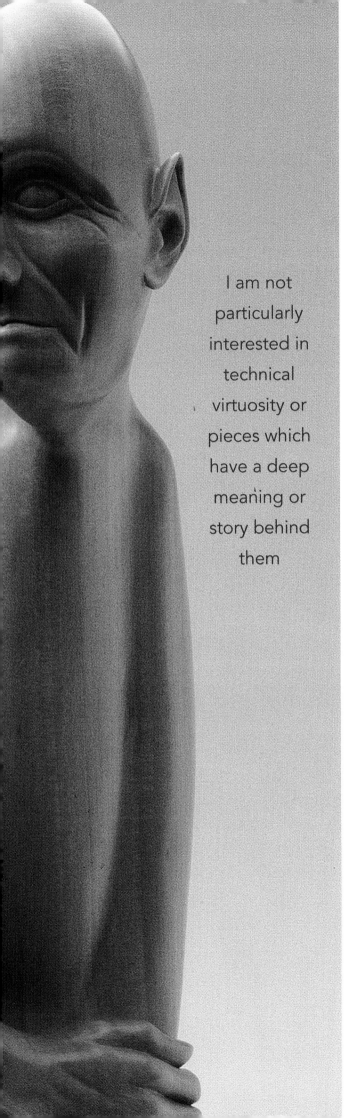

I am not particularly interested in technical virtuosity or pieces which have a deep meaning or story behind them

Man With Birds was based on two separate sculptures by American artists which feature birds in relation to man.

My sculpture had no resemblance to the work I first imagined, a simple monumental shape. Before I knew where I was, I became engrossed in the carving of his left ear, which I could not seem to sum up satisfactorily in a simple shape.

Having carved one ear in reasonable detail, the right ear could scarcely be given any less attention, but it was far less accessible as it had a bird poking in it.

In this spasmodic fashion, head and hand gained unwanted detail to produce a piece which is okay in some of its elements but, apart from a few angles, works unsatisfactorily as a whole.

A lot of my work sells in galleries within the Kent Arts and Libraries group. They have excellent facilities and insurance, and guarantee an enthusiastic and curious public will look at your work.

So far sales have been excellent. There is no money to pay up front and a manageable 20% commission. It has given me the opportunity to meet many interesting people and the confidence to know that for beginners, at least, I have something to offer as a tutor.

Cezanne painted bowls of fruit time after time to explore the relationship between shape and colour. In a similar way I do not feel the need for complicated projects or a continual search for different subject matter.

My work in future will stay simple and confident. ●

Liberon,
Mountfield Industrial Estate, New Romney,
Kent TN28 8XU. Tel: 01797 367555.

English Abrasives,
Doxey Road, Staffordshire ST16 1EA.
Tel: 01785 251288.

Cuprinol,
Adderwell, Frome, Somerset
BA11 1NL. Tel: 01373 465151.

Craft Supplies,
The Mill, Millers Dale, Buxton,
Derbyshire SK17 8SN. Tel: 01298 871636.

Terry Warren dipped out of a career as a teacher in the 1970s, choosing instead to make hand-crafted goods. He has worked with clear acrylic, hand-painted wood, and later laminated wooden jewellery which he has sold in markets and craft shops. Terry now experiments with wood sculpture as a continuation of a need to sell and stay sane.
For details of his courses, send a SAE to:
Gallery Course Bookings Secretary, Mrs Margaret Milsted, Crabble Corn Mill, Lower Road, River, Dover, Kent CT17 0UY.

LEAP OF FAITH

JEREMY WILLIAMS EXPLAINS HOW HE USED HIS IMAGINATION TO SHOW PERSONAL EXPRESSION IN HIS CARVING OF A FROG

This article covers some of the points I believe are fundamental to progress from simple and straightforward carving to individualism. This does not mean the subject itself has to be complex, nor the carving that intricate, as was certainly not the case with my frog.

I hope to show it is possible to depart from making a facsimile of a piece of work. You can incorporate your own stylistic ideas, yet still retain enough of the original subject's shape and form to make the carving instantly recognisable.

Not long ago I used this method when I was asked to carve a frog as a commemorative piece. I hope the following account will be of interest to readers, especially those new to carving. However, since much of the basic work is the same as with most carvings, I have focused on aspects which I believe a novice will find useful to follow.

Above **The finished frog**
Below **The maquette with part of the carving block behind**

I don't expect I am alone in getting a real buzz when I'm about to start a new piece of work. At this stage I am eager, I want to get on, and it is so tempting to seize a block of wood and start bashing away with gouge and mallet with little or no mental preparation.

But you do need to get mentally geared up, and over the years I have learned the success rate becomes much greater if I proceed with caution. I had not carved a frog for a long time. So I did some research first, then went on to playing about with clay.

CLAY MODELLING

Starting with clay is a method I thoroughly recommend to any beginner. It allows you to change your mind as often as you like without wasting valuable timber. You can get a real feel for the shapes you are going to produce in wood, before you do any cutting.

I have written about the use of clay models before, but I will go over the main points again. Clay lets you experiment. It allows you to introduce ideas of stylistic interpretation of the shape you may use. And if you don't care for the result when you see it in

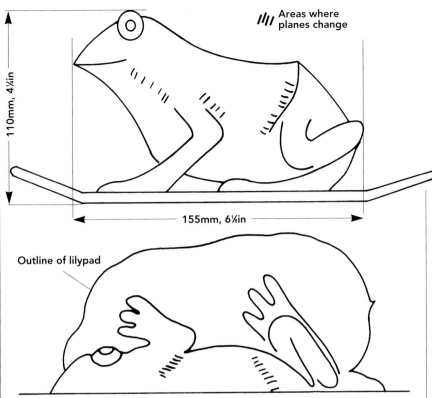

Areas where planes change

110mm, 4⅛in

155mm, 6⅛in

Outline of lilypad

Use a centre line to plot the back legs

three dimensions, no matter. Just roll the clay into a ball and start again.

But when trying out new ideas, take care what you do remains anatomically correct. In other words, avoid getting carried away into the realms of abstract too early on in your carving career.

To make the maquette (clay model) all you need is some ordinary pottery clay. This is usually cheap to buy from a local potter and will cost less than the oil-based Plasticine type you get in art supply shops. Sometimes the clay will need the support of an armature, made from wire or wire mesh, but squat subjects like my frog manage to hold themselves up without reinforcement.

Keep the clay moist, and overnight cover the maquette with a damp cloth before placing it in a plastic bag. If, when finished, you want to keep the maquette for any length of time let the clay partially harden (to leather stage) and then hollow out from underneath to prevent cracking. When totally dry, add a couple of coats of acrylic sealer to help stop the clay crumbling.

ANIMAL SPIRIT

Before making the maquette, I sourced ideas from natural history books. Then I made rough sketches to firm up my ideas. I chose not to copy any particular species, as I preferred to have the freedom of expression to capture the spirit of frogs in general, rather than getting too involved in the detail.

Working from book illustrations can make you something of a copy-cat if you try to follow them closely. I feel it is best not to be a slave to someone else's design. I prefer to look at the pictures, just to stimulate the little grey cells, then I shut the books and do some sketching. The only time I return to the book illustrations is when I get stuck drawing an anatomical feature.

To show why using a maquette is so good, let me explain what happened when I started thinking about the design for the frog. Maybe you have also experienced a mental block when trying to visualise a design shape. I certainly did with the back legs of the frog. I could see the body shape quite clearly, but I could not get in touch with the three-dimensional image of how, exactly, the legs folded, where the joints occurred.

Looking at pictures, or even china frogs, did not help that much, as some of the frogs had their legs folded one way and with others the joints were quite the opposite. In desperation I nearly took Le Shuttle to visit a Paris restaurant for a plate of frogs legs, just to find the answer!

The shape continued to bug me, and I knew I had to get it sorted out, especially as the hind legs were the key to capturing the pent-up energy that any self-respecting frog must have. It was only when I started working out the shape in clay that the picture became clear. But I must admit to

....

Plotting the shape from the maquette to the wood. Note the depth line marked on the block and the line added above it as an extra safety margin

having had a couple of false starts. Imagine, though, what the result would have been had I gone straight into carving wood. Spoilt timber and one cross carver to be sure!

SIZING UP

Before starting the maquette, it is advisable to have already selected the wood you will use. Then you will have a good idea of how big the final size can be. My clients wanted a wood with good, strong grain, so I used one of my few remaining pieces of thick elm (*Ulmus spp.*).

With the wood before me, I modelled the frog. And I estimated the carved version would be approximately 50% larger than the maquette. By making the clay model smaller than the actual size of the block, I felt certain I should have wood to spare when I started cutting into it.

Incidentally, this is where many students go wrong. They plot their drawings to the very extremities of the timber used, forgetting that curved planes (and there can be any number of them in a sculpture) need more wood for their execution than the flat surfaces. Invariably, the result is a less rounded shape than it should be. The size of the carving was not that critical, and I could make adjustments as I went along, to take advantage of the flow of the grain.

DESIGN TRANSFER

It is rarely necessary to have a maquette full-size. You can always scale up when transferring the pattern to the wood. The method for this was fully covered in issue 23 of **Woodcarving** in Jim Cooper's article *Divide and Rule*. But I did not go quite as far as he did. I worked on the basis of simple approximation, as I wished to make an original carving. And I suggest that wherever possible you try to do the same.

Don't just copy the clay model. Remember the carving will be in a

Top and above **I made sure the base was entirely flat at an early stage. The final layers of wood were removed with a chisel to avoid scoring the wood**

....

different medium to your first model. When transferring the shape of the maquette to the wood, you may need to employ some latitude of expression. For example, be prepared to make changes to make the most use of the wood's figuring. Go with the flow of the grain, and let both nature and the wood dictate the shape. Regard the maquette just as a guide.

I had two options for achieving the transfer. I could first plot the profile, cut the wood to shape, then tackle the plan view. That method would mean working with the full width of the wood to achieve the profile form.

Alternatively I could concentrate on the plan view first. There were good reasons for doing this. First, I thought it likely the frog would be viewed more from above than from the side. So this pointed to the plan view needing careful consideration.

Secondly, it was essential to have the frog well settled on to the surface of the lily leaf. Any suggestion of the creature appearing to be levitating had

to be avoided. I felt I could take care of both these better if I worked from above, rather then starting from the sides. But it is up to you which you tackle first and a lot depends on which you are happiest with.

I started by marking the upper surface of the wood with a centre line. Then I put in a centre line along the length of the body of the frog on the clay model. Both lines were then marked off with fixed points to assist plotting and transferring the design.

Those on the wood were set further apart for scaling up. These markers are useful to establish fixed reference points for measuring the body width, or to show where the body ends and the head begins. The shape was plotted by measurement, and scaled up to the size I required using dividers.

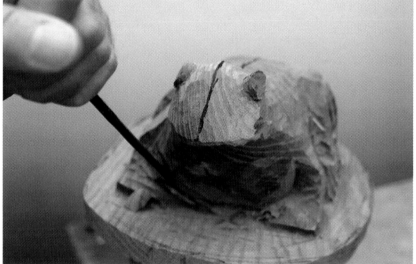

Once all the plan view detail had been applied, I took the precaution of building in two safety margins. I trenched round the outside of the design with a V-tool, making the cut in the waste wood. I then plotted a generous thickness for the water lily leaf, and added on a fraction more to take care of marks left by the saw.

WASTE WOOD

I drew straight lines around the perimeter outline of the plan view to act as guide lines for sawing off the waste wood. But one word of warning. Remember all saws leave a line of distressed wood fibres at the bottom of the cut.

These lines can be a real nuisance. They are not at all easy to eradicate during the sanding stage. You have to get rid of them early on by cutting them out, providing you have left some spare wood. So when making cuts down to wood I wished to keep in the carving, like the top of the lily leaf, I made certain I stopped the cut above the datum line.

I avoided sawing the waste down to the minimum thickness of the leaf. If I had, I would have been faced with the problem of how to get rid of the distress marks. This could have meant making the leaf much thinner than planned, and it might have started cracking and falling apart. Remember the maxim, "keep a little wood in hand, as long as you can."

SAFETY LINES

I marked on the side of the block the final depth line, and just above it the safety line. While there were still some straight sides left on the block, which could be gripped in the vice, I made sure the underside of the base was entirely flat.

If you wait until the carving is finished, then have to cope with a wobbly base, you may find there is a problem holding the carving upside down to do any planing. And if it jumps out of the vice on to the floor at that stage, it's not going to be funny.

A further precaution to take when cutting off the excess wood is not to

fully complete the vertical and horizontal saw cuts, but to remove the final layers of wood with a chisel. This way you are less likely to score the wood you wish to keep.

CARVING STAGES

There is a lot to be said for not getting locked into too much of a defined shape too soon. As previously mentioned, it can be better, especially when using timber with strong grain lines, to be guided by its flow and by the figuring of the wood, rather than to be restricted by too definite an outline.

I preferred to plot a few points to act as depth guides and then to sketch in the profile shape I wanted, again using the maquette design as a basic guide. I then roughed out the shape with a gouge, rather than relying on sawing the wood to shape.

The actual carving process was no different from any normal three-dimensional sculpture. It consisted of using a centre line to prevent imbalance creeping into the shape due to the varying density of the wood. Without it distortion can soon occur, and it is something you may not notice until it is too late. So, I made certain the line was put back just as soon as wood had been taken away.

I made most of the shaping cuts with a No. 7 gouge. This allowed reasonable quantities of wood to be removed with every stroke. Later refining cuts with a No. 4 smoothed out any undulations.

You can experience difficulty getting a good finish around areas of detail like the legs and feet when you have used too many stab-type cuts. These can so easily leave unsightly marks too deep to eradicate by normal sanding.

If you rasp the wood to take them

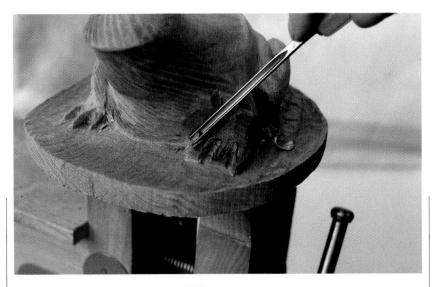

out, you are likely to leave patches of distress where you have worked across the grain, or on the end-grain, and the marks stand out like a sore thumb when the wood is polished. In places like these, cutting with small gouges is the only sure-fire way to obtain an unblemished surface.

I used a small veiner to define the outline of the legs in preference to a V-tool. It produced a softer looking cut. But a V-tool leaning over to one side is fine when you need to under-cut a small patch of shadow. Used conventionally, this tool gave a harder, more sharply defined line when marking out the feet. Convex surfaces, like the thighs for instance, were planed smooth with a chisel.

PERSONAL EXPRESSION

How you choose to express features is to a large extent a question of personal interpretation. One carver may focus on a certain aspect, yet this may be ignored by another of equal skill or experience. Frequently there is no right or wrong. You may decide to incorporate a feature just because you like the idea, because it pleases you, and nothing more.

On other occasions, though, there may be a specific reason for departing from life-like reality. For example, in the pictures you will see I built a ridge into the body above the hind quarters, and mirrored it by the definition of the body line reaching the forelegs. Both features were exaggerated from those in the maquette.

I also made a ridge along the length of the spine, although in reality this should have been a hollow. Stylistic changes have to have a purpose. When I saw how the look of the wood developed as it got smoother, I felt the surface finish could be enhanced by not having such a plain, rounded shape.

It seemed more spectacular to break up the body line by introducing secondary planes. These would create more interest, afford a greater play of reflected light and, by the way they caused the grain to bend, enhance the effect of the patterns in the wood.

I also opted to make the body surface plain, which helped to make it quite clear that this frog was a smooth-skinned genteel frog, not a rough and warty toad.

FINISHING

The finishing stages involved planing the convex surfaces with a chisel, and taking paring cuts in the hollows to smooth the wood as much as possible. Some of the final shaping was done by sanding, using Hermes 406 blue J-Flex abrasive wrapped round cushioned sticks.

I strengthened the visual impact of the eyes, outlined in shape with a half-round No.9 gouge, by dotting in the pupils using a nail with a rounded tip as a punch. I shaped the water lily leaf forming the base with a coping saw.

Then I lightly ripple cut the surface with a small No.3 to provide visual contrast to the smoothness of the frog. The edge of the leaf was rolled to the underside to give some lift, which helped to lighten the look of the carving. I treated the whole carving to three coats of Liberon finishing oil. Each coat was buffed with a Webrax pad when dry, and finally waxed.

Commission work can be taxing, as you can never be entirely certain how the piece will be received by your clients. Thankfully mine seemed pleased with the carving, and paid up happily. Or perhaps they were just very polite people! ●

Liberon are at Mountfield Industrial Estate, New Romney, Kent TN28 8XU Tel: 01797 367555

Jeremy Williams started carving at the age of 14. He has extensive experience as a teacher, and runs his own courses on woodcarving. He contributes to several woodworking magazines and has also written a book, *Decorative Woodcarving*, published by GMC Publications.

SHAVE THE WHALE

RAY WINDER SHOWS HOW TO CARVE A HUMPBACK WHALE

This is a simple project for carving a humpback whale which should be fun and within the capabilities of all carvers.

You will need a blank of lime (*Tilia vulgaris*) or similar wood, a few simple tools, some abrasive paper and finishing materials.

Start by sawing out your blank to the shape of the drawing with a bandsaw or coping saw. You can make the blank any size you want. Mine was about 14 x 5½ x 1½in, 355 x 140 x 38mm.

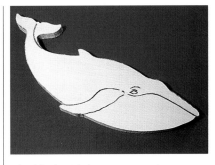

The blank with features traced on.

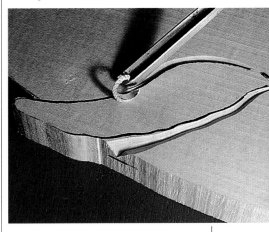
The finished whale on its stand.

I used three chisels, a 12mm, ½in No 3 fishtail, a 6mm, ¼in No 8 and an 8mm, ⁵⁄₁₆in V tool. A small mallet is useful when using the V tool.

I also found a scalpel fitted with a 10a blade invaluable. It was excellent for fine detailing and getting into difficult areas.

Of course you may use other chisel sizes if you find them more appropriate or convenient and they do the job. Power tools with rotary burrs could also be used.

You may also find a small rasp useful for final shaping and removing chisel marks before working through the grades of abrasive papers.

The blank can be fixed to a piece of scrap wood with double-sided sticky tape, and the scrap clamped to a bench or table. The smoother the piece of scrap, the better the tape will grip.

Adjust the plan drawing to the size you want. The easiest way of doing this is with a photocopier. Tape the drawing to your blank and trace the position of the fin, eye, mouth and tail-ridge line using carbon paper.

The throat furrows are marked later after the throat has been carved and sanded smooth.

FIRST CUTS

With the V tool cut a groove following the lines either side of the large fin starting at the eye end. Use a mallet if you feel it gives you more control of the cut.

The depth of the groove at the start of the cut should be no more than 2mm deep, but as the chisel moves towards the tip of the fin it can get progressively deeper.

As it reaches the edge of the wood the groove should be just under half the thickness of the blank.

You may find it easier not to attempt this in one deep cut but to remove wood at the side as shown in the photographs, and then gradually take the groove deeper.

Use the 12mm, ½in fishtail to remove waste, starting at the fin and moving along the throat of the whale and up to the mouth.

The groove for the large fin is cut with the V tool. Note how it deepens towards the outer edge of the blank.

The direction of the chisel is pushing from the body of the whale outwards towards the edge with a slight sideways twist taking small cuts.

Check the curve of the throat by studying the cross sections on the plan drawing. Note the curve of the throat begins just below the mouth line.

After roughly rounding off the tip of the nose, the mouth is re-drawn and the V tool is used to cut the line back in.

The whale's belly can now be carved in the same way as the throat, only working back from the fin to the tail this time.

Look at the cross sections drawing again to understand the curve required. This time it stops at the midway point between the belly and the back of the whale.

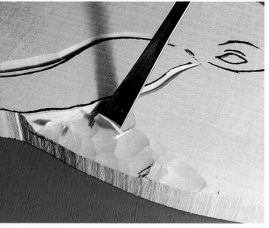

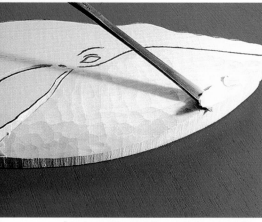

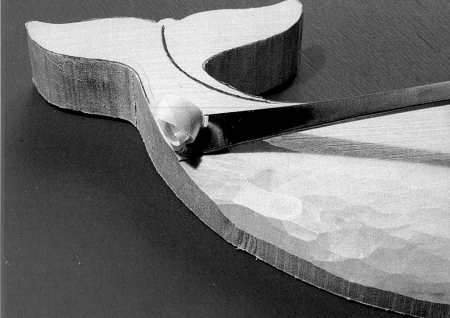

Top **Removing wood at the side with the fishtail chisel.**

Cente **Removing waste from fin to mouth with the fishtail chisel. Note the direction of cut and sideways twist taking small cuts.**

Above **After rough shaping the mouth is re-drawn and cut in with the V tool.**

Top right **Carving the belly, working back towards the tail.**

Above right **Note where the curve stops midway between the belly and the back of the whale.**

The tail flukes are carved using the 6mm, ¼in No 8 chisel. The photos show this in progress, working down from each side of the back line.

Note the tip of the left hand fluke is 6mm, ¼in below the original surface of the blank. This depth can be marked and the wood reduced to this level with the fishtail chisel before shaping the flukes.

The finished shape of the tail flukes is best seen in the photographs of the completed carving. Study these carefully for best results.

BACK

Next carve the back of the whale using the 6mm, ¼in No 8. Working from the tip of the nose back to the tail, the cuts are made across the grain towards the outer edge.

The tip of the small dorsal fin on the whale's back can be cut to within 6mm, ¼in of the back board. When sufficient wood has been removed the fishtail chisel can be used to smooth the area into a flowing curve.

I used a scalpel fitted with a 10a blade to shape the eye. First make a vertical cut around the drawn shape of the eye, then carefully make angled cuts around the inner edge to leave a slightly domed eye.

The eyelid ridge above the eye can also be defined and rounded over with the scalpel.

This is a good time to turn the carving over and carve the back of the fins and the tail flukes.

The whale can be prised off the

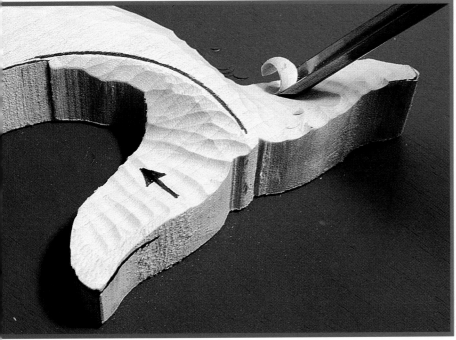

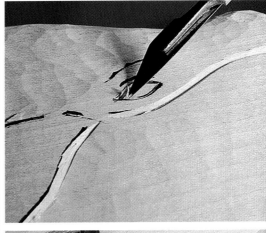

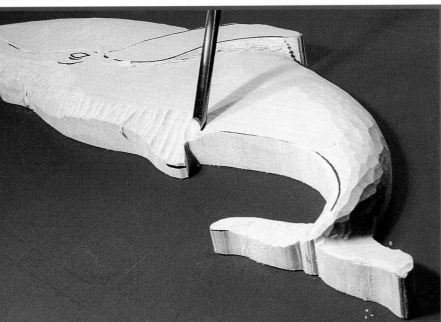

Top **Carving the tail flukes with the 6mm, ¼in No 8 chisel.**
Above **Carving the back of the whale, working from nose to tail.**
Top right **Cutting out the eye with a scalpel.**
Centre right **Shaping the fin. Keep enough thickness to avoid breakage.**
Above right **The throat furrows are carved with the V tool after sanding the area smooth**

....

back board by carefully sliding a knife under it, hopefully leaving the tape stuck to one of the surfaces.

Holding the whale down temporarily with tape or a clamp, cut away the waste at the back of the large

fin by making a series of vertical cuts down with the fishtail chisel and then cut in horizontally until the two cuts meet.

The fin can then be shaped more fully. Note it gets thinner towards the tip but still has enough thickness to avoid it being liable to breakage.

The plan drawings show the final shape of the tail flukes and the small dorsal fin. These are carved first with the 6mm, ¼in No 8 and then smoothed with the fishtail chisel.

Again leave a reasonable thickness of wood to avoid any possible breakage. Once you are happy with these areas sand them smooth and turn the carving back over.

If the double-sided tape is still clean you should be able to re-position the carving back on the base board ready for finishing.

I found it easier to sand the throat area first, and then mark the furrows running under it using the plan drawing as a guide.

GROOVES

Use the V tool for cutting the grooves, taking care to get them starting and finishing in the same place. Use a small mallet if you feel it gives you more control of the cut.

The raised area between the cuts should have their edges rounded over to soften the furrows.

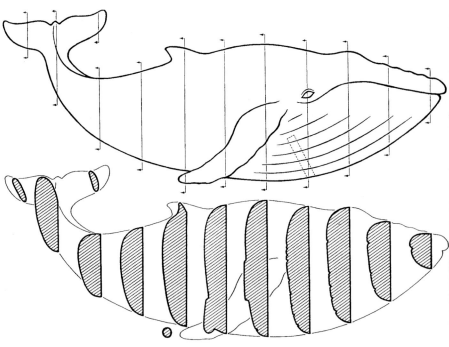

Front of the finished whale mounted on a rod.

Above **Whale outline and cross sections through the body.**

Note also the rear edge of the large fin is carved to taper back slightly.

The carving is now ready for final sanding. You can use a small rasp to remove chisel marks and blend the curves into a smooth shape.

I started with 100 grit cloth-backed abrasive and worked through the grades to finish finally with 500-600 grit. There are no really sharp edges that can be over-sanded, but take care around the eye.

It helps to glue strips of abrasive to flat and shaped sticks to help in obtaining a ripple-free surface without low spots.

Sanding can be a slow and tedious process, so be patient if you want a really scratch-free surface.

Before waxing, seal the wood with sanding sealer or several coats of varnish thinned around 60/40 with white spirit. Wipe it on and off with a cloth to avoid a heavy build up. Lightly sand between coats with a fine or worn piece of abrasive paper before finally applying a wax polish.

The wood will eventually darken to a mellow golden brown colour.

You can mount the whale on a metal rod, and to do this you will need to drill a hole in the body. The angle for this hole is shown on the plan drawing.

Use a wooden base (I used oak) with another hole drilled to take the rod. ●

BIRDS OF A FELLA

Keith Pratt tells Nick Daws of his fascination for carving the graceful lines of birds

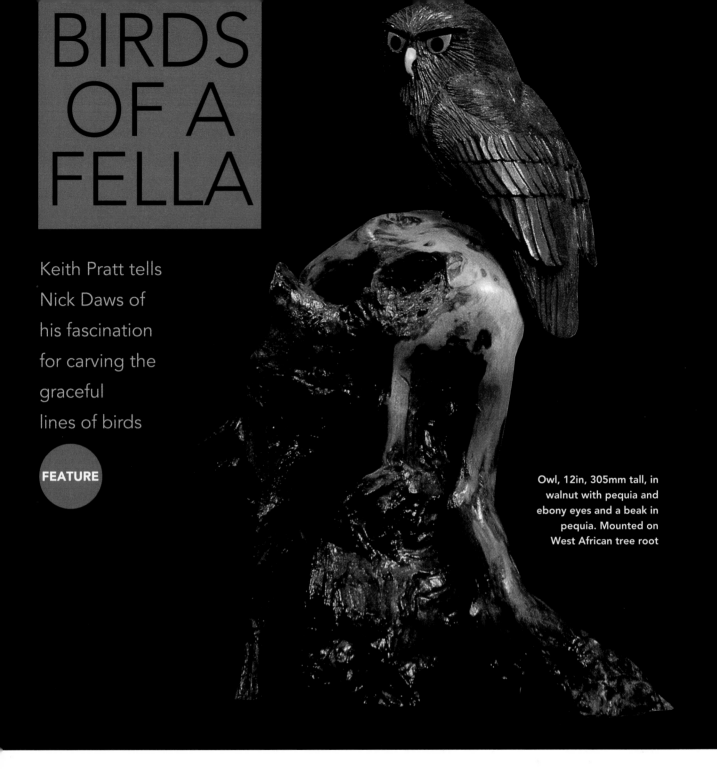

Owl, 12in, 305mm tall, in walnut with pequia and ebony eyes and a beak in pequia. Mounted on West African tree root

B irds are my favourite subjects. I've tried other animals such as foxes and otters, but I've never been entirely happy with the results. I keep coming back to birds. They have a line about them which I find attractive and graceful. I always use walnut (*Juglans spp.*) or ebony (*Diospyros spp.*) for the main body of my birds. Walnut is my particular favourite, partly because of its colour and texture which suit the subjects very well. It is also a well-behaved wood. You can carve with, across or against the grain. It won't lift or split, and because it's so hard you can get very fine detail.

I use ebony for its colour. It's a difficult wood to carve, but the finished result is spectacular. I've tried other woods in the past, such as danta (*Nesogordonia papaverifa*), a close-grained smooth form of mahogany, but I didn't much like it and you can't get it in sufficiently large blocks. I've also tried Honduras mahogany (*Swietenia macrophylla*), but I've always gone back to walnut and ebony.

I never paint my carvings, as I prefer the natural colour of wood. Because of this, I have to use birds which are easily identifiable by their shape, such as kingfishers, hawks, blackbirds, wrens, owls and shags.

I've been asked to do a hedge sparrow, but unless you do the carving and paint it, it's hard to tell the difference between it and other small birds such as the yellowhammer. I carve birds you couldn't mistake for anything else, which are also nice to look at.

Personal interpretation

When I'm carving a new bird, my first problem is to get the design right. I use a photo or drawing to get the basic outline, and work from there. This is a personal thing, and it can take a long time for me to arrive at something I am happy with. It took me 18 months to get the shape and size for the blackbird, for example.

It's clear what my carvings are, but I don't aim for anatomical perfection. The finished article is a shape which pleases me and, hopefully, the public. You could say, to some extent, they have become caricatured, but in a very subtle way.

Once I have got a two-dimensional outline, I draw it on the block of wood. I always use the end-grain of the timber, as this gives the finished carving a more rounded look. Then, using my Al-Ko bandsaw, a very useful and almost vital tool, I cut it out using either a ⅜in, 10mm and or ¼in, 6mm blade.

The width, or depth if you prefer, is something I have worked out over the years by trial and error. I draw a centre line around the block, and using gouges, get it down to the approximate shape I want. The gouges I use are ⅜in, 10mm and ¼in, 6mm No.5, ¼in, 6mm No.11, ³⁄₁₆in, 5mm No.9, and ⅛in, 3mm No.6.

I sand down to a smooth finish, ending with 180 grit sandpaper. At this point, I carve out the eye socket using a ⅛in, 3mm No.6, ³⁄₁₆, 5mm No.9 or ¼in, 6mm No.11 gouge depending on the size of the bird, and drill a hole for the eyeball.

Developing detail

The feathers are done using ³⁄₁₆in, 5mm, ¼in, 6mm and ⅛in, 3mm No.39 v-tools. This takes a long time, and the tools have to be constantly sharpened and buffed up. I get a good mirror finish using jewellers' rouge on the usual leather strap. When carving the primaries and secondaries of the wings, I lay the chisel on its side to create the long impressions. For this, it is crucial the tools are kept razor sharp.

Wren, 5in, 125mm tall, in walnut with ebony eyes and pequia beak. Mounted on West African tree root

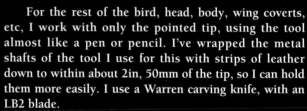

For the rest of the bird, head, body, wing coverts, etc, I work with only the pointed tip, using the tool almost like a pen or pencil. I've wrapped the metal shafts of the tool I use for this with strips of leather down to within about 2in, 50mm of the tip, so I can hold them more easily. I use a Warren carving knife, with an LB2 blade.

The beak is fitted in a v-shaped slot cut out in the bird's head and glued using PVA adhesive. It's essential it fits exactly. I leave it to set for 24 hours before carving it into shape.

The eyes are usually made from an ebony dowel rounded at the outer end and glued in place. The exceptions are owls, hawks and blackbirds, where I use pequia (*Aspidasperma spp*) drilled down the middle and fitted with an ebony centre dowel. The eyes are then cut off in slices, with one side rounded. When the feathering, eyes and beak are all finished, the whole piece is sealed with a wood sealer, gently rubbed down and polished with beeswax polish.

The base is as important as the bird itself

Photos by George Huxter

It's clear what my carvings
are but I don't aim for
anatomical perfection

**Kingfisher with wings folded, 10in, 255mm tall.
The body is in walnut, eyes ebony, beak teak.
Mounted on yew tree root.**

The base

The base on which I mount the birds is as important as the bird itself. I use old tree roots which I find in the woods, preferably yew (*Taxus baccata*), but basically anything I come upon and like.

If I find a very nice piece, I might take it to a sandblasting firm to have it cleaned up. Mainly, though, I do this myself, using wire brushes of various sorts. A flexible drive on an electric drill comes in very useful here. When the whole root is clean, I seal it in the same way as the bird.

To mount my birds, I use an aluminium rod ⅛in, 3mm in diameter, together with resin glue. I put the two pieces together by hand to see where the bird is going to sit. Then I drill the bird and the mount to take the rod, and glue it into place. Once the glue has almost set, I bend the rod into perfect position for the finished effect.

Including both the bird and the mount, the wren took me about eight hours to do. The kingfisher with folded wings took 16, and the flying kingfisher about 30.

I work in the back garden of my home, in two sheds battened together for the purpose. It's not exactly spacious, but it suits me fine. The tools I use are fairly conventional, but I don't use a normal woodcarver's vice because I find they don't hold the wood steady enough.

Keith Pratt in his workshop

My vice

The vice I use is a converted Black and Decker Jobber, a small version of the Workmate, mounted on a large block of wood with a bolt through the centre and bench. This allows me to rotate it for ease of access to the carving. It holds the wood rock steady, so I can get more detail into it. The jaws of the vice are lined with ¼in, 6mm thick leather.

I plan to concentrate on my existing repertoire of about 10 different birds. That may sound unadventurous, but I do them all in slightly different ways, and they're constantly improving. I want to try some different attitudes, showing the birds in flight and with wings half-open, for example. Some time, I'd also like to try a much bigger bird, such as a life-sized sparrowhawk.

I still get a lot of pleasure from carving something as small as a wren, and I'm glad to say the public seems to share my enthusiasm. After seven years as a full-time woodcarver, I'm still pleasantly surprised people are willing to pay me for something from which I get so much enjoyment. ●

Keith Pratt can be contacted for commissions on 01243 373714

Shag, in ebony with pequia eyes and beak. Mounted on West African tree root

Blackbird, 8in, 200mm high

PROJECT TIMELY GIFT

SOME JOBS JUST WON'T BE RUSHED, AS BILL MANDER FOUND OUT WHEN TACKLING A CARVING OF ST JOSEPH THE CARPENTER

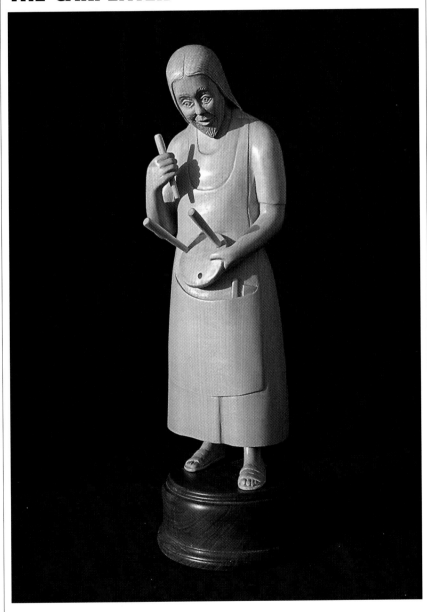

St Joseph with the final base.

I was quietly working away on a carving of *St Joseph the Carpenter* on the Berkshire BWA Group's stand at the Newbury Show last summer when somebody asked how long my carving would take.

The answer was difficult to find, because when I came to think about it, it had been a very long time.

The idea first came as a request from the mother of a friend in a local choir. She was looking for a woodcarver to carve a figure for her church. I said I was interested and thought no more about it.

About a week later I received a telephone call from London. The caller said she was pleased I was willing to do this carving for her, and she described her idea to me. Her daughter was to be confirmed soon and her parents wanted to present the church with something to mark the occasion.

The parents had a particular idea in mind, a figure of St Joseph the Carpenter, set so he was looking down at the viewer, almost as a friend or teacher. I could also think of the viewer as their own daughter. Here indeed was a challenge.

PLANNING

The next stage had to be a visit to discuss my approach to carving, and to look at the setting for the finished work. It was also for me to say whether I was interested in the project.

This is a stage I always find fascinating, checking out the idea against the problems involved, the size, the time-scale, the techniques to be used and how the job fits in against other pressures on my time.

The visit also involved going to the church and imagining how the carving would appear to someone sitting in one of the pews. The idea was to have Joseph looking down upon the daughter and her family. This required drawings, measurements, and some careful checking of angles and heights.

Finally we came to discuss the timing of the project. Luckily there was no great urgency, although they wanted to present the carving before the daughter's confirmation became a distant memory.

After an extensive discussion we agreed I should take on the project and would begin with some designs and research on suitable blocks of wood.

Above **Preliminary sketches.**

The finished statue should be about 610mm, 2ft high.

MATERIALS

The discussion of woods was interesting. The husband came from New Zealand, and his occupation caused him to visit his home country frequently. They liked the idea of using wood from that country, so we decided to look for something light and fine in colour and grain.

Within a couple of months I received a parcel containing a sample of kauri (*Agathis Australis*) and a paperback on Maori carvings. This was a bonus.

Also included was a photograph of the timber mill where the wood had come from, with a workman supporting a large block of kauri. I am afraid this produced a disappointment, as when I started carving into the sample attempting some detailed features, the wood split and the detail quickly disappeared.

I believe the sample was not suffi-ciently seasoned. With much regret we decided we could not risk the same thing happening with a much larger block of kauri so we settled for English lime (*Tilia vulgaris*). It is a pity, as I would have loved to have used a new and unusual wood.

Bill Mander carving Joseph at the Newbury Show.

Above **The final design.**

SETTING

During the search for an appropriate wood I was also busy planning designs for the carving. I had left the church with an impression of the setting and its relationship to the viewer.

The figure of Joseph would be at eye-level to an adult standing, and well

Above **Close up of figure.**
Above centre **Front/face of figure.**
Above right **Side view of figure (right side).**

above anyone sitting in the pews. They wanted him looking down at their daughter, so the position and the direction of his eyes was very important.

I produced several drawings of a carpenter working at his bench, and immediately there was a problem with the angles involved. The bench at which he was working blocked out at least half the figure.

The original idea which I had agreed with the family had to be changed to bring the figure into view, without a bench. Actually the new concept seemed more suitable, as there was no distraction from the gaze of the carpenter.

The parents agreed the new designs, with the figure standing looking down at their daughter and putting the finishing touches to a stool he was making.

I had to do some research into the clothing worn by craftsmen of that time. There did not seem to be the present concern for health and safety. Today we would be concerned about the length of hair and the protection of the feet, but the sandals won the vote.

The wood was to be lime, which gave me an excuse to visit The Working Tree, and enjoy a country break. A piece the size I required, 600 x 300 x 200mm, 24 x 12 x 8in, was not available, so I had to settle for two 100mm, 4in lengths and some very

careful joining. Luckily the grain and wood colouring blended in well.

I drew the design onto the three surfaces of the made-up block, and removed the waste around the figure. The lack of a bandsaw meant a more time-consuming method of removing unwanted wood. I used a handsaw to make deep cuts into the waste and a broad gouge to chop it down to the drawn shape.

CLAMPING

The method of holding the block presented problems as the waste was removed. Eventually I had to screw an additional block onto the base and clamp it into the vice. Only when most of the waste had been removed did I transfer to my carver's clamp.

I left the area below Joseph's gown until most of the area above was ready for finishing. As I worked on this section around the feet I began to see the balance of the figure was not quite right. He was in danger of falling over.

I therefore decided to cut off the left leg well above the ankle and, using a dowelled joint, moved it forward to bring the foot outside the dress line. This gave a more attentive look to the carpenter, with a slight forward lean.

The right hand and arm had to be shaped to hold up the stool leg, while the seat was carved to be held against the apron. The three stool legs were made separately and glued into place.

FRENCH CHALK

The finishing of the figure was time consuming. I started the fine shaping with a range of rifflers. I then turned to a varied range of abrasive papers, ending with a fine flour finish.

During this period I tried to keep the surface as clean as possible, with French chalk dusted onto my hands. When this was completed I wiped the wood clean with a tack cloth and gave it several coats

of white sealer. Finally, this was rubbed back gently and wax polished.

One decision still remained concerning the shape, height and colour of the base. The choice was walnut (*Juglans regia*), stained darker to give a contrast to the figure. I tried several free-formed shapes, which were eventually rejected for the taller, turned form.

The polished figure of the carpenter was then attached to the base. This was done by drilling and countersinking holes through the base and then gluing and screwing up into Joseph's legs. Provision was made on the base for a plaque to be placed by the family at the time of the presentation to the church.

After a period that must have covered nearly two years the family came to collect the carving. The most satisfying moment of all that time was when the 12-year-old daughter gazed at the carved figure of St Joseph for the first time. It made all the planning, the designing and the long hours carving well worthwhile. ●

Bill Mander, 66, retired from teaching eight years ago. His leaving presents included a set of woodcarving chisels and several books on carving. He taught art and design, and his family had a woodworking background.
His work has ranged through a variety of themes and has involved both abstract and realistic approaches. As a member of the British Woodcarvers' Association he has produced carvings for several of their projects including *Shakespearean England.*
He has also taken on the organisation of the Berkshire Group of the BWA and would welcome contacts from any other woodcarvers working in the Thames Valley. Tel: 01734 478425.

Award-winning bird carver Paul Kedwards describes the inspiration and techniques behind his glossy sculptures

WILD AT

People often come up to watch me working on carvings at exhibitions, and probably the question I am most often asked is "How long does it take?" I am apt to reply, with tongue in cheek, "40 years", as I feel my style has evolved over a lifetime's work.

I believe it is necessary to know a subject intimately, as only by acute observation can a successful carving be achieved.

Although I have won many awards for my life-size sculptures of British birds, including Awards of Excellence at the National Exhibition of Carved Birds at Pensthorpe, Norfolk, I feel I am a very down-to-earth craftsman.

If you ask me what has influenced my work, I would probably reply "Old Rolls Royces". Subtle lines, smoothly running curves and a wonderful finish characterise my work, but a lifetime's observation of wildlife and a familiarity with their anatomy are also very important.

I have to capture the jizz of my subjects, perched on ledges, clinging to a wall, or balanced on slender legs.

I was born in 1941, in Sutton Coldfield, Warwickshire. I grew up, the youngest of four brothers, in a home full of animals and birds. These included a pair of magpies, a pair of jackdaws and a squirrel, all of which had fallen out of their nests.

We also kept tree frogs, snakes and pheasants, as well as the more usual companions.

Love of the outdoors

All of us boys spent a great deal of time in Sutton Park, which adjoined the garden. This was a wild area of woods, bogs, lakes and grassland, a paradise for young lads, and it gave us all a lifelong love of the outdoors.

Top left **Paul Kedwards with his award-winning mahogany carvings of a common tern and a cuckoo with a reed warbler.**
Photo courtesy of the Leicester Mercury.
Top **Long tailed tits.**
Above **Common tern.**
Above right **Pair of little owls.**

I yearned to find a more artistic career, and collected together a folder of my drawings. Having boldly introduced myself at a Birmingham advertising agency, I was taken on as a somewhat mature studio junior.

Four years later I moved to a large international company in Leicester as a lettering artist. Lettering, another of my passions, requires the same discipline and temperament as wood sculpture: strict rules interpreted with some flair and flourish, and the ability to see round corners!

By the end of a long career with the company I was responsible for display production for hundreds of nationally known High Street shoe shops.

I have always enjoyed working with wood, designing and producing my own fitted kitchen, wardrobes and a large rocking horse for my daughter as well as carving birds and animals.

My first exhibition was undertaken in 1975, without much enthusiasm, as a favour to a friend who wanted an additional attraction at a local flower festival.

The exhibition was a total sell-out and brought further offers of local exhibitions. I have subsequently had shows in London, York and Warwick.

My work has frequently been displayed at the art exhibitions staged as part of the RSPB annual members' conferences.

Self-taught, I use traditional methods and old hand tools to create each piece. About half the time a sculpture takes is spent after the basic shape is achieved, meticulously rubbing down and polishing to produce the smooth, glossy finish which is my hallmark. This shows off the curves and razor edges typical of my work.

Hardwoods

I have used many hardwoods, including elm (*Ulmus spp.*), walnut (*Juglans regia*), teak (*Tectona grandis*) and rosewood (*Dalbergia spp.*), but I am drawn to mahogany (*Swietenia macrophylla*) for many reasons: its strength, the wonderful feel and smell, superb colour and grain.

Its unique tiger's eye appearance is created by the tree's spiralling growth, which is clockwise one year and anti-clockwise the next. Thus the grain runs in two directions and is a continual challenge to carve.

When planning a carving I make numerous drawings of the intended subject in various poses. Having chosen one, I carefully select a piece of mahogany from my stock. For small birds, this comprises old doors, table legs or bank counters from architectural salvage yards, really old, fine quality wood.

HEART

My parents, both art teachers, encouraged my interest in drawing the wildlife all around us, and I was often at the kitchen table carving animals and birds from soap and blocks of salt provided by my mother.

However, I always felt misplaced in an academically inclined grammar school. There, artistic ability was rather discounted, and working with your hands most certainly frowned upon.

One double period of art a week was never enough, and so I entertained my classmates by drawing through maths, Latin and history too.

At one point a timetable choice had to be made between art and woodwork, and for a change I chose the latter. Thus began my association with wood. I carved animals and birds, the subjects I knew best, giving them away to friends.

I left school with some O levels but, to the horror of the staff, opted to enter a trade, and took up ironmongery.

After two years it was evident I was not cut out to be a salesman so I left, but in that time I had gained a craftsman's attitude towards tools, which has been of inestimable value and interest ever since.

As each sculpture is made from one solid block, careful consideration is given to the way the design can be placed on the wood so delicate features are carved with the grain.

I often lick pieces of mahogany to ascertain what the final colour will be when polished, although I can usually judge by the weight. Heavy mahogany is always dark, a piece light in weight is usually light in colour.

Sketch plan

The next step is to trace the drawing on the selected piece of wood and bandsaw out the profile. I then sketch a plan onto the cut-out profile and cut this out either by bandsaw or by hand, using a bow saw or coping saw.

Depending on the size of the piece, I then start carving the corners away using either a recently acquired flexible drive machine with rasps, or conventional chisels. Whichever way I start I always use my Addis chisels to achieve the final shape.

Right
Cuckoo with reed warbler.
Far right
Barn owl.

I take ripped off pieces from a roll of 100 grit belt sander and start rubbing by hand to smooth the work down. By the time the polishing stage is reached I will have used 220, 400 and 800 grit wet and dry paper, all by hand.

When I am completely satisfied there are no imperfections in the curves, I put the carving in the sink and pour boiling water over it, immediately fishing it out and letting it dry. I then rub it down with 1600 wet and dry (two 800 sheets rubbed together).

The boiling water treatment raises the grain, so any subsequent application will still leave the wood smooth.

When all the hard work has been done, linseed oil is applied to the carving, which gives the wood real life and depth.

Linseed oil

Without the use of the oil, I believe French polished mahogany can look uncannily like a synthetic wood laminate. What matters to me is the feel and look of a natural material of great worth and beauty.

Having allowed the linseed oil to soak in for roughly two days, I then paint on a thinned down solution of sander/sealer. This seals the wood and acts as a barrier between linseed oil and French polish.

Having rubbed the sander/sealer coat down with 220 grit paper, a coat of 50/50 sander/sealer and French polish is brushed on, allowed 24 hours to dry and again rubbed down.

Subsequent coats are applied in the traditional manner of a cotton wool pad inside a piece of linen dipped into French polish, with only a very small amount of linseed oil dabbed on to stop it from dragging.

This is where patience is required, waiting for each coat of French polish to dry before rubbing it down to apply the next.

The weight of the wood does give an indication of the colour of the finished carving, and some very hard pieces of Brazilian mahogany only require two coats, while some very light African pieces need 10 or 12 coats before I am satisfied the depth and colour of the wood have been fully revealed.

When I feel the polishing is complete, I pour a little Brasso into my cupped palms and walk round the garden, fondling the finished sculpture in my hands until the surface is glass-like.

When the weather permits I often work outside with my Tiranti woodworker's vice set up on a Workmate in the garden. This is surrounded by large trees, abounding with squirrels and a huge variety of birds, giving ample opportunity for observation at close quarters.

I like to feel I am a very discriminating craftsman, and my own severest critic. If a piece does not satisfy my standards it never sees the light of day.

I find my work appeals to art lovers and birdwatchers, lovers of wood and craftsmen, and anyone interested is welcome to visit me to see the current collection.

Three dimensional silhouettes was a recent observation from a friend, and it sums up my sculpture perfectly. ●

Paul Kedwards,
44 Forest Rise, Kirby Muxloe, Leicestershire LE3 3HQ.
Tel: 0116 239 4203.

Addis tools available from Proops Brothers Ltd,
24 Saddington Road, Fleckney, Leicestershire LE8 8AW.
Tel: 0116 240 3400.
Alec Tiranti Ltd, 70 High Street, Theale,
Reading, Berkshire RG7 5AR.
Tel: 0118 930 2775.
Workmate made by Black & Decker Ltd,
210 Bath Road, Slough, Berkshire SL1 3YD.
Tel: 01753 511234.

PROJECT SLIVER ME TIMBERS

DON POWELL CARVES A POPULAR FICTIONAL CHARACTER FROM HIS CHILDHOOD

him as having a face as big as a ham when the cabin boy, Jim Hawkins, first meets Long John Silver in the Spyglass Inn. I spent some time researching pirates, although my original cover was the most interesting.

A 610mm, 2ft length of white beech (*Gmelina leichhardtii*), about 125 x 180mm, 5 x 7in was planed square and appeared tight grained, clear and faultless. It had been stored by a prominent local cabinetmaker friend for about 20 years.

The original drawing.

I have always had a fascination for characters from the books read in my childhood, and have carved a few of them.

I've had a copy of *Treasure Island* since I was nine or 10. The book has a fine cover illustration by G.P. Micklewright with Long John Silver in the foreground.

Although I had been intending to carve it, a client's enthusiasm made the project irresistible.

The illustration depicted the pirate half turned. In sketching a front view I did change a few minor details, but I was determined to retain the alert, suspicious expression on his face.

Robert Louis Stevenson described

The figure bandsawn from a block of white beech.

UNDERSTANDING WOODCARVING IN THE ROUND   25

I pinned my sketch of the front profile to the block and traced it with carbon paper. I then bandsawed this profile and attached it by its base to a ball socket vice for carving.

I did not cut a side profile but used my sketch on the block to locate key points on the figure as I removed excess wood with my chisels to provide a rough form of the figure.

During the course of the carving I made a couple of changes. The first was when I came upon a check in the wood where the bird was to be situated. It was like a fissure inside the timber.

Above **The figure roughed out.**
Below **The face and hands further detailed.**

Below **Back view showing detail of the gun mechanism.**
Below right **Pistol, buckle and button details emerging.**
Right **The lamp carved separately and fixed initially with wire.**

Applying detail to the macaw.

BIRD

I opted to carve the bird separately in boxwood (*Buxus sempervirens*). This is one of my favourite woods so it gave me a good excuse and opportunity.

My plan was for a rope in Long John's hand as in the original illustration, but I finally opted for a lamp. This had to be carved separately as I did not have enough material, having planned for a rope.

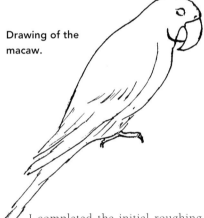

Drawing of the macaw.

I completed the initial roughing out leaving clumps of wood to accommodate the hands, the top section of the crutch, the musket and the pistol. The rough shaped face signposted the nose, eyes and mouth.

Smaller items like buttons and straps were marked with a dot of green marker which reminded me during the course of the carving to allow for these details to appear later.

Not being a mental giant in the field of memory I find it helpful to signpost these smaller details, as it is easy when working progressively over and round the piece to forget and carve away an area where a particular detail is situated, leaving the area too shallow to provide a convincing item.

Working over the piece for shape and form I used a full length mirror in the workshop, checking my own image complete with reversed broomstick for the crutch, to visualise the three-dimensional figure being uncovered from the block.

If you cannot visualise the form, it is useless to cut away blindly expecting the piece to materialise as if being beamed up by Scotty in Star Trek.

At this point I carved the face to a more advanced stage. I raised the brim of the hat to better expose the face and shaped the structure of the face with smallish chisels.

EXPRESSION

I then clarified its details with finer gouges, knives and a micro scorp, paring the wood away to define the expression I required. A slightly surly, tough and suspicious appearance was what I hoped to achieve.

I then shaped the hands and crutch before clarifying their details using a mirror.

At this point the carving was well on its way and required a methodical and careful approach, continuously working over the whole figure fashioning the shapes and clarifying the detail.

I carved the lock mechanisms with reference to the weapons of the era, and after shaping with very fine knives and gouges, cleaned them up with a diamond tip ball in a Dremel.

The cutlass was fashioned after the short weapon of the seafarers of the era.

I carved the lamp separately from a suitably small length of white beech held in a vice until the base was finally cut away.

I drew the design directly onto the wood and roughed out with chisels. I finished the windows with a bent No 2.

I fitted the lamp for trial with wire, then replaced the wire with a carved wooden handle. To fashion this, I laminated six layers of white beech veneer crossing the grain, and cut it out with scalpel and Dremel with a fine tungsten burr.

I used a riffler for final shaping, then the piece was sanded and sealed with a varnish type sealer. The finished piece had enough flexibility to be sprung into position into the hand after threading through the ring top of the lamp.

Next I carved the bird, a macaw. I transferred the side profile to a small slab of boxwood and bandsawed it using a clamp to hold the wood safely. I then held this profile in a small modeller's vice and roughed it out with chisels.

FEATHERS

I detailed the feathers with a scalpel, then finished off the bird in the hand using micro gouges, scorp, knives and rifflers. I tooled it over carefully and finally buffed it over with a cloth buff in a Dremel.

I carved the macaw with reference to numerous photographs and artwork on the subject. Apparently the macaw is highly intelligent, so I shaped it to be peering round into Long John's face.

I prepared his shoulder for the bird by carving the coat to convey the slight impression of claws. I then

The macaw fixed in position on Long John's shoulder, peering into his face.

Above **The lamp with wood handle, crutch and macaw all fixed in place.**

drilled the bird and shoulder to accept a metal supporting rod and epoxyed it into place.

I carved the bottom length of the crutch and jointed it separately, otherwise a huge block of wood would have been required for the project.

I used a length from the original source and sawed and carved it to shape with a knife before fitting and epoxying it using a metal pin for supporting strength.

I took care to ensure the added section was jointed to conform to the line of the top section.

The base was carved from a block of white beech reclaimed from an unfortunately demolished Queensland historic house. It was probably about 90 years old, a young house by British standards.

I cut this piece to 230 x 230 x 140mm, 9 x 9 x 5½in thick and carved it to portray a sandy surface. I embellished it with a buried treasure chest (partly uncovered), and a skull.

The idea was the pirate who buried the treasure killed the digger to keep the location secret.

I drew the position of the chest on the block and then roughed out the area around it with a large gouge leaving a small mound for the skull.

Above **The base with sand, chest and skull carved from a block of reclaimed white beech.**

I carved the surface undulating to assume the appearance of sand. I detailed the chest to leave it half exposed, and the skull using either a real skull or a replica from an art suppliers as a model.

BASE

I then cut Long John from his base, positioned him on the new base and shaped the surface to achieve the appearance of his crutch and foot sinking into the sand.

The final fitting entailed the use of carbon paper to form a neat join before the foot and crutch were epoxyed into place and reinforced with a sturdy screw through the base into the leg.

I sanded the piece to a fine finish paying particular attention to ensure detail remained clear and sharp.

My object was to produce an antique appearance with colour, depth and a nice lustre.

I stained it with a diluted oak woodstain applied with a 50mm, 2in square of sheepskin, then rubbed it down with Penetrol using a lint-free rubber.

I applied about six coats, wiping excess off carefully and allowing each coat to dry thoroughly. I applied the final finish of Danish wax with 1200 wet and dry paper.

I mounted the piece on a base of 32mm, 1¼in Jarrah (*Eucalyptus marginata*) which presented a pleasing contrast. I stuck felt on the bottom to protect any fine surface it may be placed on.

Above **The foot and crutch screwed from underneath to the pre-shaped base.**

I hope my efforts will prove to those carvers casting about for subjects for projects, that young peoples' literature provides a fertile field for ideas. ●

Dremel Multi power tool available in the UK from Robert Bosch Ltd, PO Box 98, Broadwater Park, North Orbital Road, Denham, Uxbridge, Middlesex UB9 5HT. Tel: 01895 834466.

Don Powell was born in England but moved to Australia when he was 11. A career with the Queensland Police Force gave him contact with many and varied characters and developed an eye for detail.
In retirement he has developed his childhood interest in carving and has visited Europe and Britain to study the works of great sculptors. Last year he won a travel scholarship to study sculpture and visited Switzerland, Germany and Britain for a course with Ian Norbury. Don now runs The Image Maker Workshop in Brisbane where he teaches and carves commissions.

HOLY ORDER

MICHAEL HENDERSON EXPLAINS HOW HE MADE A CROSIER FOR THE BISHOP OF SWINDON

The dove and crook after finishing

I designed and made a Crosier for the Bishop of Bristol 10 years ago. Last summer, the Bishop phoned to tell me a new Bishop of Swindon was being ordained. He asked me if I would like to make another Crosier.

The appeal of doing work for the church is joining a long tradition, which goes back to the Medieval and Gothic period. Then, design and craftsmanship were integral, and together they developed the technology and art to produce structures and spaces of great beauty. The builders must have been very different from us and yet we find it easy to appreciate their creations.

They worked the stone by hand and lifted it into place with their own muscle-power. This gave them an intimate knowledge of the material and its strength as a space containing substance. Into this space they placed portrayals of the occupants of their world, earthly, divine, or devilish. They had no inhibitions about the way they carved these figures.

In the Gothic period, the relation between the spatial and sculptural achieved a balance rare in the history of architecture. So I was glad, if a bit awed, to be asked to add a new Croiser to the end of this tradition.

THE BRIEF

The Crosier is a Bishop's ceremonial staff, about 6ft, 1.8m tall. The design brief was to produce a Crosier with a carved top in oak (*Quercus robur*), which would unscrew and pack away in its own box, then fit into the boot of a car. I had to produce the design and work out the costs.

Usually a Crosier is in the shape of a shepherd's crook. A Bishop is Christ's representative and Christ said "I am the Good Shepherd." We decided to put a dove on the crook, representing the Holy Spirit.

The round top of the crook would contain the dove. It had to fly downwards, as the Holy Spirit is given from above. The vertical element of the staff emphasised this, a little like a lightning conductor.

The dove was planned as a two-sided relief. The staff was in three sections, the bottom two turned and screwed together to the top one, like a billiard cue. It was carved from one solid piece, and underneath the dove was a Bishop's mitre and a crest identifying the Diocese.

DESIGN

I had to play with geometry to make this work. The circle of the crook had to be the right size proportionally, and to

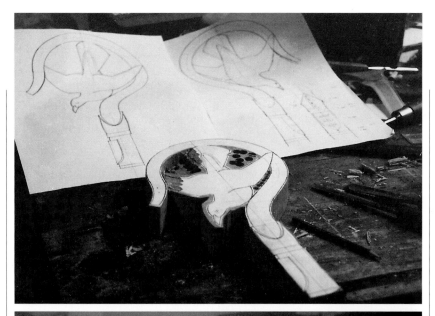

contain the bird. This had to appear to fly freely, at the right angle, and yet be attached in sufficient places to be strong.

To give the dove depth, each wing was designed to touch opposite sides of the crook. The whole Crosier had to have the right taper to look elegant and the parts had to fit into the box in the most space-efficient way.

I did some half-scale drawings for the Bishop, which he liked. He makes decisions in moments and is an excellent man to work for. Then I did a detailed drawing of the taper for the turners, who looked worried by it.

A modelmaker designed and made the fittings beautifully in brass. English oak was bought from Wessex Timber and a woodworking shop machined the oak section for the sides of the box. So all the components of the project were ready.

CARVING STAGES

I stuck the design to the wood and sawed out the top section. It was a pierced relief with no background. I drilled piercing holes cautiously to allow some extra wood for the development of the shepherd's crook and bird. This was to ensure they would look the right weight and touch in the right places.

Carving alternately from either side of the work, I formed the wings and tail so they passed through the circle of the crook, being attached to either side of it. This gave the bird the appearance of flying in a horizontal plane and required the further away wing to be smaller. Viewing the Crosier from both sides meant this smaller wing alternated. This was possible because part of each wing was hidden behind the crook.

I carved the breast to touch lightly on the first bend of the crook. Then I incised

Top left **The crook is roughed out and piercing holes drilled**
Left **Michael starts to chisel out the waste**

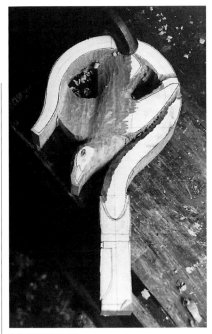

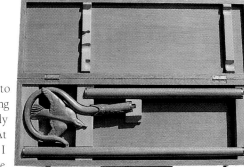

the feathers to contrast the wing from the body and crook. At the same time, I developed the crook section from a round to almost rectangular shape at its end. This created a lovely space in which the bird could fly. I carved the crest and checked the diameters so they would marry with the lower sections and fittings.

FINISHING

I sanded the whole Crosier and varnished it with satin acrylic. I centred the brass fittings, checked the Crosier for straightness when assembled, and glued and screwed the fittings.

When I had made the box to contain it, I carved bearers for the top and bottom so when it was closed the three sections were held snugly in place. The box had brass hinges, a leather and wood handle and briefcase clips. After it was varnished, I rubbed down all the oak lightly and gave it a wax finish.

It looked very smart. The brass fittings on the Crosier were substantial and yet did up in a few turns. The assembled Crosier was straight and the tapers looked right. It all packed away nicely into the box.

I delivered the Crosier on a golden autumn afternoon. The new Bishop of Swindon was ordained in Southwark Cathedral the following Sunday.

The Bishop of Bristol was very pleased. Walking down the hill afterwards, the world felt good to me, every leaf on every tree looked in just the right place. ●

Above **The dove is roughed out**
Below **Front view of shaped dove and crook**
Below right **Rear view of shaped dove and crook**
Above right **The finished Crosier packs away neatly in its box**

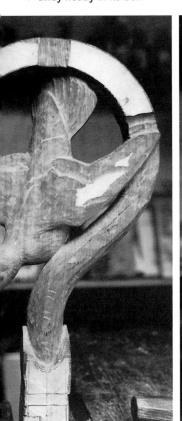

Michael Henderson can be contacted for commissions at Bristol Craft and Design Centre, 6 Leonard Lane, Bristol, BS1 1EA

Michael Henderson was born in Scotland, the son of an engineer. He studied architecture and, while in Indonesia, was influenced by the view of sculpture as both spiritual and functional. He moved to Bristol in 1983 to concentrate on woodcarving, and his work is now exhibited and sold widely. He describes his approach as having a Scottish engineering foundation with an Oriental superstructure.

PROJECT

WHERE EAGLES DARE

PHIL TOWNSEND DESCRIBES HOW HE ROSE TO THE CHALLENGE OF CARVING A LIFE-SIZE EAGLE

Until recently, I have concentrated almost entirely on relief work, so I was confronted with quite a challenge when commissioned, at short notice, to carve a full size eagle in-the-round. I have been carving more or less full-time for the past five years and knew eventually I would have to get to grips with in-the-round work on a larger scale than mantlepiece-sized stuff.

When I was asked to carve this eagle there was a kind of fear barrier to be broken because it had to be done in just over three weeks, which left little or no time for making major boobs. I knew it was going to be a case of making it up as I went along, never having tackled anything quite like it before.

My client had been inspired by a rare imported carving he'd seen in the entrance of a local bowling alley. It was carved from one solid block of some unknown South American hardwood and stood over 4ft, 1.2m tall.

I was shown photographs of the sculpture and asked if I could do something similar. I said I thought so, but added it would not be cut out of one solid block. I had neither the necessary timber, nor the means with which to waste out such a chunk. And so started a small voyage of discovery which, although it had its anxious moments, eventually landed me and my client at the desired destination.

I decided to use lime (*Tilia Vulgaris*), partly because I had some boards in stock that might be up to the job, but mainly because I didn't want to add to my problems with tough or tricky grained timber.

My second decision was to make the wings separately and joint them to the body. I took three views of the bowling alley eagle – front, side and back, and scaled them up to full-size as outline drawings on a large sheet of paper. I traced the profile of a wing from the drawing on to a 1½in, 38mm board and added a couple of inches (around 50mm) at the base for a tenon joint.

To aid uniformity, I made sure I could get both wings out of the same board by cutting out the first on a bandsaw then using it as the pattern for the second.

WOOD WEIGHT

There were a number of aspects to this carving which I would change if asked to do a second version. One would be to use heavier timber for the wings. At the time those 1½in, 38mm boards seemed thick enough to provide curve to the wings. Indeed, at 12in, 305mm

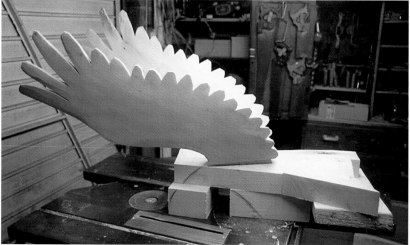

Top left **The wing pattern is taken directly from the drawing and copied for the other wing**
Left **The wings are shaped and tried in the mortices to check the pose**

wide and about 36in, 915mm long I was wondering how the short stub tenons I'd allowed for were going to support their weight.

I should have realised, after carving, their weight would be only a fraction of the original, with the lightest area being at the wing tips and the heaviest and strongest at the base.

With hindsight I would have used 2in, 50mm or 2½in, 63mm timber for the wings as this wouldn't have added to the finished weight, but would have enabled me to shape them more dramatically in their depth. An eagle's extended wings form something of a slow spiral which is intrinsic to their beauty.

In the event, I made the most of the material I had. I rough-shaped it with a Lancelot chain cutting disk in a 4½in angle grinder so the tips of the uppermost primary feathers (at the front edge) and those of the feathers closest to the body (at the back), literally 'feathered' off to the outer edges of the wings.

LAMINATION

With this stage done, and feeling more confident, I turned my attention to the much more complex business of laminating up the body shape. I had some trouble visualising how this was to be built up but as time was of the essence, I decided to get going and modify or add bits if necessary later on.

The original lamination was made up of four pieces: a main one (pre-chamfered to take the wings), a second to give fuller body and the tops of the legs, a third for where I thought the head might be, and a last, thinner board for the fan of the tail.

Two double-pronged mortice slots were designed to take the tenons on the wings. They were cut at an angle to the line of the laminations, and on the chamfered faces, to impart a greater sense of life. To counter-balance this, I set the tail in the reverse direction, which is why an extra triangular piece has been glued to the side of the body.

VISUALISATION

Next, I dry-fitted the wings to the body to help visualise the bird and sketched pencil lines on to the side as an indication of the finished profile.

After I had added a second trian-

Above left **The line of the legs is drawn onto the side to test the balance of the bird**
Above centre **Rough shaping the bird while clamped to a table**
Above **Shaping the head**

gular piece to the other side of the upper part of the tail, I used the Lancelot disc again to effectively rough carve the upper face of the tail fan. I smoothed out the slight hills and hollows with a coarse (36 grit) sanding disc, pencilled in the tail feathers and profiled their tips with a coping saw.

I sawed off the block on the underside at an angle and, with wings in place, sat it on a table edge to visualise the bird's pose once again. The pencil line indicated how the top of the legs might look, but I decided the body section between the leg block and the head was too thin and in-filled it with another small lump.

This resulted in end grain joint lines, which are weak and difficult to do without being noticeable. This was another area for improvement given a second opportunity.

After I glued on an extra block to

The base is built up with separate blocks

extend the legs, I began carving the primary and secondary tail feathers. I used the square and parallel faces of the underside block to clamp in a vice. This proved effectively solid for working both above and below the feathers.

Next, I added a further piece to the head to give the eagle the extended, reaching pose I had in mind. Using the 'leg' block clamped end on to a table this time, put the carving in a better position to rough out the head. I sketched a rudimentary eagle's profile onto the head and then began carving in earnest, tapering off the beak and deeply insetting the eyes.

CREATING REALISM

The carving wasn't based on any one type of eagle but was intended to portray the essence of an eagle in all its fierceness and wildness. To that end, the beak was carved so the upper and lower bill were separated and pierced through above and below the tongue, which seems to be almost hissing a warning to the viewer. But I left the

tips of the bills joined for strength.

With head and tail three parts carved, it was time to consider the balance of the carving and how its weight was to be supported. With wings fitted, I rocked it gently on the back edge of the leg block until I found the point of balance.

Using a bevel gauge to determine the angle between the block and the horizontal, I sawed a lump of lime to that angle and wedged it underneath. This wedge-shaped block would become the perch on which the eagle would land.

I gathered a variety of off-cuts to build up a pile of 'rocks' underneath the bird, sufficiently high to give the tail feathers good clearance. To increase the realism of these rocks I carved and assembled them individually to give maximum visual interest. I then glued and screwed them into the monolithic whole.

Now the base was finished, I sat the eagle on it once again and realised I had made the legs too short. So I glued and screwed rounded blocks, representing the ankles of the bird, to the underside of the leg block. The screws were later removed. Again, I used the flats on the block sides as a holding

point while I worked on the legs and breast. I kept the feathering on these areas simple, using scooped cuts.

Then I roughly cut a pair of feet on the bandsaw, joined at the inner toes, and placed them beneath the ankles, which had been slightly offset to increase the twist in the pose. But my twelve year old son thought the eagle looked more interesting when stood on tip-toe.

I carved the feet separately from the rest of the bird, then drilled through the centre and temporarily screwed them into position.

I had to make the feet fit properly on to their rocky perch. To increase the sense of them gripping onto this foothold, I altered both of the rear talons and one of the outer front ones so they curved around the edges of the rock.

Below **The wings are glued and jointed into place and feet are screwed and glued to the legs**
Below right **The completed carving prior to staining**
Right **Rear view showing feather detail and slow spiral in the wing profile**
Far right **The head and tail feather tips are left unstained**

proud. With the heads of the screws removed, these acted as steel dowels which located in holes bored in the rock at the points which I had previously marked.

The completed carving stood 45in, 1145mm high and weighed around 45lbs, so it was helpful to be able to move it around in two pieces. I transported it lying, with feet in the air, on the back seat of the car and delivered it just, but only just, in time for Christmas.

All in all, the piece had worked out well and I had covered a lot of ground in the process. But I don't enjoy cutting things quite so fine (no pun intended) and it was with some relief, the following day, to be carving the turkey instead. ●

Phil Townsend's work in high relief has won awards in the International Woodcarvers Congress two years in a row. He usually works in this medium because he believes it allows for a broader choice of subject matter. The manipulation of a limited depth of wood to give the appearance of full 3D is the technique which most intrigues him. He can be contacted for commissions on 01833 640683

ASSEMBLING PARTS

Now it was time to fit this large three dimensional jigsaw together. The wings, which I had fully carved in the interim, were glued into their mortices. Here was another area for improvement. If I had left a deeper shoulder on the tenons, ie made the tenons a little thinner, there would have been greater leeway in carving around the joints after the wings were in place. This would have increased the sense of realism.

I glued the feet to the legs, removed the screws and replaced them with dowel points. I then positioned the eagle on its rock and pushed the points into the surface. I put a second pair of much longer screws in the feet with about 2in, 50mm of shank left

ODMEDOD'S EXPRESSION

THE SCARECROW AS A PASTORAL PACIFIST? ANDREW THOMAS SUBVERTS A RURAL ICON

If I have achieved the intended result, the theme of this carving should speak for itself. Briefly, Odmedod is an enlightened scarecrow who has witnessed humanity's greed for money and the lengths to which we are prepared to go in order to obtain more.

With this awareness, he has rebelled against his primary function, pulled loose from his restraints and joined forces with nature to share peace, love, friendship and equality.

If I covered every detail involved with this carving I would half fill the magazine, so I have concentrated on the most important and interesting techniques, which can also be adapted to your own ideas.

Initially, I played around with the idea on paper, drawing rough sketches until I felt the balance and pose were correct. I then had photographs taken of myself, wearing a big overcoat, baggy trousers and hat. I held this pose from four different angles: front, back and both sides.

The photographs were then enlarged, using a photocopier, until the side view measured 100mm, 4in at its widest point, which was the maximum available depth of kiln dried American black walnut (*Juglans nigra*).

I traced the right hand side and front profiles, modifying them to match my drawings. These tracings gave the correct dimensions necessary for carving, and for the profiles to be drawn on the wood for bandsawing.

MATERIALS

I obtained my wood from Yandle & Sons of Martock, who have a good selection of timber.

The main body, hat, crow, hand restraints and fox were made from American black walnut: 610 x 200 x

....

Figure 535mm, 21in high in American black walnut, English lime, English walnut, African blackwood and Australian grass tree root.

Left **The birds and other details are fixed in place with rods and epoxy.**
Above **Rear-view of the figure starting to take shape.**
Below **From the front, the clothes are becoming better defined.**

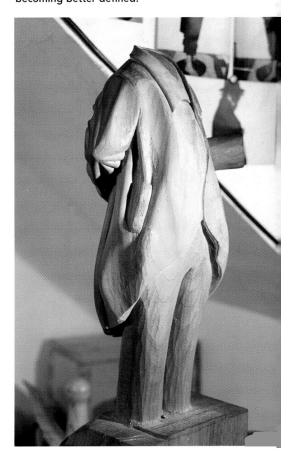

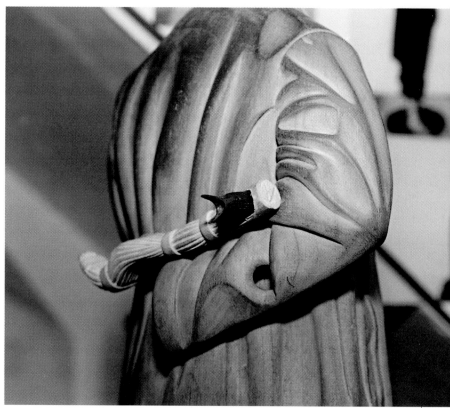

100mm, 24 x 8 x 4in.

The head, hands, feet, seagull, badger and cross were of English lime (*Tilia vulgaris*): 610 x 152 x 75mm, 24 x 6 x 3in.

The peace dove and chick nesting in the sleeve were from African blackwood (*Dalbergia melonoxylon*): 100 x 50 x 50mm, 4 x 2 x 2in.

The umbrella was of English walnut (*Juglans regia*): 127 x 50 x 13mm, 5 x 2 x ½in.

And the base was made from Australian grass tree root (*Xanthorrha preissii*): 280mm, 11in in diameter.

All these materials were kiln dried and selected for their suitability for the subject, strength and matching colour tones.

To enable accurate bandsawing, I planed the wood flat and square. Using the traced drawings and carbon paper, I drew the front and right side profiles onto the wood.

The first cuts on the bandsaw were along the sides of the body from the top view, approximately 1.5mm, ¹⁄₁₆in outside the line, the waste wood being taped back with masking tape, to keep the block square.

Next, from the side view, the front and back were cut 1mm outside the line. I left a small block of wood 152 x 100 x 75mm, 6 x 4 x 3in at the base of the bandsawn figure. This was used for mounting the figure onto the faceplate and vice.

Using drawings and photocopies as guides, I drew the seam (edge) of the coat onto the wood, starting at the collar, then down across the stomach and round the back of the legs.

The chisels and knives I use are Swiss made by Pfeil, whose numbering system varies from the traditional

Sheffield list numbers.

I started the carving using a 20mm No 5 straight sweep to round off the lower edge of the coat. Then with a 10mm V-tool, I cut along the coat seam from the opening on the stomach, over the trousers and around the back of the leg.

I pared back the trouser side of the V-cut with a 10mm No 5 straight sweep. I repeated this process, lowering the trousers slightly each time, until they appeared to be naturally going up into the coat.

Moving onto the legs, I used the 10mm V-tool, chip carving knife No 1, 5mm and 10mm No 5 straight sweeps to cut in between the legs to separate them, then rounded them off to their approximate shapes.

Next I tackled the top half of the body. The first point to remember was the scarecrow would be looking at his left hand held out to his side. This would naturally alter the angle of the upper torso, making the left shoulder go backwards and the right shoulder come forwards at approximately 15–20°.

Using a 20mm No 5 straight sweep, I carefully cut away the front of the left shoulder and the back of the right shoulder, viewing from the top, until the correct angle was reached. I then matched in the angle on the other side of the shoulders and the rest of the torso, gradually straightening out as I

got nearer to the waistline.

Next came the basic shape and positioning of the arms. Using my drawings and photocopies as measurement guides, I drew the outlines of the arms onto the wood. I then carved them to their correct widths and depths, using a No 1 chip knife, 10mm V-tool, 10 and 20mm No 5 straight sweeps, and 15mm No 7 straight sweep.

MODELS

When trying to recreate real life, intense studies must be made of every detail. I always gather as much helpful information as possible from books, magazines, videos etc. If you have a PC with a CD Rom, a fantastic amount of software is available on all subjects.

With this particular project, using my wife as a model was very useful, as it gave a clear view of all necessary information, resulting in good, life-like balance, form and detail. If finding someone to model presents problems, a dressmaker's dummy can be modified as a prop for the correct hang of overcoat and trousers. Use your initiative!

My folds were exaggerated, giving the desired fantasy effect with striking shadows. Personal taste dictates how much is done to the clothing.

Attention must be given, though, to the parts from where the folds radiate, the shoulders, elbows, knees

Far left and left **The arm is inserted up into the sleeve and the chick with the 2mm rod glued into it, goes through the arm and approximately 5mm into the wood behind holding everything in place.**

and crotch are the main centres.

The tools I chose for the clothing were: Chip carving knife No 1, straight sweeps: 2 and 5mm No 2, 10 and 20mm No 5, 4, 8 and 14mm No 7, 5mm No 8, 5 and 12mm No 9, 1, 2 and 5mm No 11, 1 and 10mm V-tool.

The most awkward part of all was the removal of wood from the back of the coat, going up behind the legs to the buttocks. For this task I used 5 and 12mm No 9 straight sweeps as far as I could go, then changed to rotary burrs.

For the carving, I used 8 and 10mm spheres and 6mm tapered, tungsten carbide cutters. For cleaning up, I used a 6mm sphere and 4mm tapered diamond burrs.

The techniques used for making holes in the sleeves, trousers and neck were the same. I used a 10mm brad pointed wood bit, set my drill to a slow speed and drilled the holes to the correct angle, approximately 50mm, 2in deep.

Then, using a 10mm sphere, tungsten carbide cutter, I enlarged the openings of the sleeves etc., cutting back in an inch or so, giving a natural view up inside, but leaving the last 25mm, 1in untouched.

This would be where the dowel on the end of the arm, neck or leg would be jointed and glued. If rotary burrs aren't available, the same effect can be achieved by using 5 and 10mm No 9 straight sweeps.

The making of the hands and feet was based on anatomy and scale. With the aid of books, I made drawings onto limewood and then bandsawed them out. I drew a 10mm, ⅜in circle on the ends to be doweled and used a chip knife to round off the edges of the last 25mm, 1in, until it fitted tightly into the drilled hole.

Again using a chip knife, I rounded off all the hand and foot edges, until the basic shapes could be recognised. I used an 8mm No 8 straight sweep to slightly hollow the palm.

I cut out the hand and foot bindings with the knife, making quite a deep slit, then pared away the adjacent wood, leaving the bindings standing proud. When all the bindings were completed, I sanded over the entire area, excluding the dowel, with 120 grit until everything looked correct.

I cut grooves approximately 2mm, ⁵⁄₆₄in apart all the way round the limbs, hands and feet using a 1mm V-tool, giving the appearance of straw.

REFERENCE POINTS

As the head was an important feature of the carving, I took great care in planning each stage. I used front and profile passport photographs of myself which I enlarged to the correct scale on a photocopier.

I then traced them, altering the mouth and nose, and tilting down the angle of the profile, so the head would appear to be looking down towards the hand.

I followed the same procedure for bandsawing the head as for the main body. Carving the facial features was really not too difficult. I drew a line down the centre of the face on my drawing and wood, and marked reference points along this line, between eyes, tip of nose, top of lips, chin etc.

I measured from the reference point out to the widest part of the features using a vernier gauge, and marked it, repeating the process for the opposite side.

Using the profile drawing, I took measurements vertically back and marked them from the same reference points. These gave the correct width and depth from which to work. A profile gauge can also be very helpful and time saving, to check the depths match accurately on both sides.

To remove the waste to the correct depth and to carve the features, I used chip knife No 1, straight sweeps 2 and 5mm No 2, 10mm No 7, 4mm No 8, 3 and 5mm No 9 and 1mm V-tool.

I used the knife for most of the waste removal and detail as it was invaluable for producing the deep slits round the eyes, in between the lips and hair line etc. For the neck dowel and straw hair I used the same procedure as for the legs and arms.

WILDLIFE

The birds were fun to plan and make. I followed the same procedure as earlier, with scale drawings and bandsawing. I researched in books to find the correct shape of wings, feathers, undercarriage

etc. The chip carving knife was again used for most of the work.

I marked out the position where the peace dove and chick were to be fixed on the right arm. I used a 4mm brad pointed wood bit to drill the hole and offset with a tapered ruby rotary burr. This connected with the hole drilled up the sleeve. I then inserted the straw arm up the sleeve into its correct position.

I copied the shape of the hole in the coat onto the arm, then drilled it out and shaped it in the same way, taking great care to drill only about 5mm, ³⁄₁₆in deep. I drilled 2mm, ⁵⁄₆₄in holes with a HSS bit, 5mm, ³⁄₁₆ into the back of the chick, through the centre of the hole in the arm and approximately 5mm, ³⁄₁₆ in the wood behind.

I cut a 2mm, ⁵⁄₆₄in brass rod to size and inserted it into the back of the chick, through the arm and into the wood behind, holding everything firmly in place.

I drilled the dove's beak and the chick's throat using a 1mm HSS bit, to a depth of approximately 5–8mm, ³⁄₁₆–⁵⁄₁₆in. Then I made a tiny crevice to match the shape of the dove's beak in the back of the chick's throat with a tapered ruby rotary burr.

Above **The head, like other extremities is carved in detail beneath the outer clothes.**
Below **Selection of sticks made and used for sanding awkward areas.**

I cut a 1mm stainless steel pin to size and inserted it into the beak of the dove, which I then, in turn, inserted into the chick's throat. This resulted in a good, natural, flush finish, with no sign of the pin protruding.

All parts of this carving, including those attached with a pin and rods, were glued with epoxy resin.

Sanding such a complex carving required many hours of patience and attention. To help myself with this task, I made a selection of small, wooden sticks. These were cut on the bandsaw to the applicable width and depth and were 152–178mm, 6–7in long. The ends were cut to the required shape and angle with a chip knife. I then cut sandpaper to match the end of the stick and stuck it on with a small drop of instant glue, trimming away excess paper before use.

I used aluminium oxide sanding sheets, grits 120, 150, 220 and 500 for sanding all areas. I applied linseed oil to the wood, imparting a natural, deep, rich colour. After several days I rubbed over the carving with 0000 wire wool, and applied several coats of Briwax, to achieve a good, smooth but not too shiny finish. ●

Yandle & Sons, Hurst Works, Martock, Somerset TA12 6JU. Tel: 01935 822207.

Pfeil tools available from Craft Supplies, The Mill, Millers Dale, Buxton, Derbyshire SK17 8SN. Tel: 01298 871636.

and Tilgear, 69 Station Road, Cuffley, Herts EN6 4TG. Tel: 01707 873434.

Andrew Thomas was born in 1963 and lives in Dorset. His career in woodcarving started 12 years ago, when he bought and restored a traditional horse-drawn bow top caravan. During the recession Andrew decided to become a full-time woodcarver. He is virtually self taught with the aid of books but some years ago, attended a short course by Ian Norbury. The inspiration for Andrew's work stems from his deep, personal feelings about life in general and the various global events and ecological problems that have occurred during his lifetime. His work has been successfully exhibited in county and national competitions.

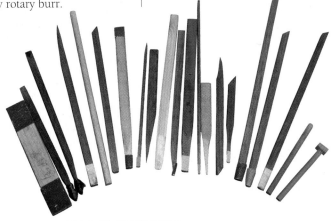

HORSE SENSE

RAY WINDER DESCRIBES HOW HE CARVED A HORSE HEAD SCULPTURE FOR A BANGKOK BUSINESSMAN WITH SEVEN BROTHERS

The brief from my client for this sculpture was relatively simple, but it took a lot of scribbling and rejecting of ideas before I came up with a design I felt worked.

The Bangkok businessman who commissioned the carving was born in the year of the horse and had seven brothers. He wanted these elements incorporated into a wood sculpture in the form of eight horses that in some way appeared to be moving forward into the future.

A little research into traditional Chinese sculptures soon confirmed a feeling I had that the horses should be depicted as powerful, aggressive beasts with flared nostrils and bared teeth. With only vague concepts for designs, I thought it might be useful to check my stock of wood for the largest useable pieces of English walnut (*Juglans regia*) (I had at least decided on what wood to use).

....

The completed carving

I had some large chunks chainsawn from a tree that had come down in the 1987 storm. One piece in particular looked promising being around 28in, 710mm long, 19in, 485mm wide and 8–9in, 200–230mm thick.

Although I was able to use the full length due to remarkably few drying cracks, I had to cut some soft, wormy sapwood away to leave around 7–8in, 180–200mm thickness and a width of around 16–17in, 405–430mm. For its size, it appeared to be as well air dried as you could expect.

CONCEPT

My initial thought was to make the piece as a relief, but as I had such a

seven smaller horses and then lower the surrounding area accordingly.

DRILLED HOLES

I initially concentrated on the left hand side of the head, the eye being the first important point to be established. The area behind the cheeks and chin also had to be cut away in order to shape the head. I drilled a series of holes through from both sides until they met in the middle. This made it much easier to remove waste wood.

With the left side of the head roughly shaped it was time to shape the right side to match. To do this I fixed a board temporarily to the bottom of the carving. On to this board I drew a series of numbered parallel lines. Using these lines as registration marks, I was able to measure a point on one side of the horse head and transfer it to the other using a home-made pointing device.

This process may sound rather involved, but if the object being carved is symmetrical I find this technique quicker in the long run, and certainly more accurate.

Having got both sides of the head roughly balanced in relation to each other, I removed the board for conve-nience and began defining the main facial features on one side, such as eyes, nostrils and lips, sanding each area as it progressed. Once I was happy with one side, I fixed the 'pointing'

large, thick block available, the concept slowly evolved of one large horse head with the other seven heads 'growing' out of the neck in high relief.

When I had a final drawing I was happy with I sent a copy to the client for approval. Once I had the go-ahead I enlarged the drawing to fit the block of wood and transferred the outline on to it.

The first stage was to run the wood over the planer to give a flat and true edge to work from. I cut the outline of the large head roughly to shape with an electric chainsaw as the wood was far too heavy and awkward to bandsaw.

I had a good idea in my mind of exactly how I wanted the main horse head to look: a short muzzle, flared nostrils, mouth open with bared teeth, generally stocky and powerful with perhaps slightly stylised and exaggerated features rather than an elegant, realistic head.

With a centreline marked down the nose and along the neck, I started removing the waste with an angle grinder and carving disc. With the occasional use of the chainsaw, wood was quickly removed until the neck tapered back and I was able to mark the outline of the

Top left **With the main features of the horse head carved, the seven smaller heads were outlined and the surrounding area lowered**
Centre left **Holes were drilled through behind the cheeks and chin to make waste removal easier**
Top right **A board was fixed temporarily under the head so reference points could be marked for the other side**
Above **The main facial features were completed on the front side**

board back in place and accurately transferred the final measurements across to the other side of the head.

Although areas such as the inside of the mouth and the teeth still had to be worked on, I felt it was time to

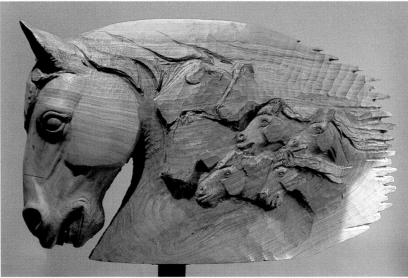

Above **With the front side completed, measurements were again taken using the board to complete the rear**
Above right **Much time and care was needed to get proper overlapping of the seven smaller heads**
Below **Detail of the overlapping heads, further refined**
Below right **The carving was supported on blocks so the base could be roughed out before being fixed on two gold plated brass rods**

⋯⋯⋯⋯⋯⋯⋯⋯⋯⋯⋯⋯⋯⋯⋯⋯⋯⋯

concentrate on the neck and the seven small heads.

It was necessary to study real horses and as many photographs as possible for this carving, although there are so many different kinds of horse with their own differing facial characteristics, I thought it better to concen-

trate on their expressions rather than identifiable breed types.

HIGH RELIEF

The smaller heads were in quite high relief, so time and care was needed to work out the relative positions of the heads, with much adjusting needed until they overlapped comfortably.

I wanted the neck end of the carving to finish as sharp, aggressive, almost windswept points formed out of ridges and ripples that flowed through from the horses' manes. I hoped this would create the impression of movement.

I had decided at the initial design stage the base should be a slab of oak (*Quercus spp*) shaped to follow the curve of the horse's neckline. It was necessary to temporarily support the head on the

roughed out base to gauge and mark this curve accurately. The almost completed head was supported on wooden blocks while this was being done.

The finished sculpture was eventually supported on two rods. These were ¾in, 20mm brass that I had gold plated to avoid any future discolouration or tarnishing.

The final sanding of a piece this size is very time consuming. I worked through progressively finer grits finishing with 600 grit.

I always like to oil walnut, in this case with a generous coating of boiled linseed oil which darkened the wood and brought out that deep rich colour. Once this was dry I applied several coats of Danish oil which sealed the wood, and I was then able to finish the carving with a wax polish. ●

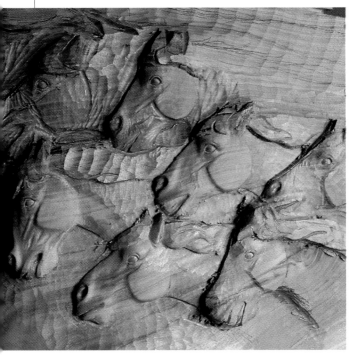

MIGHTY MOUSE

LEE DICKENSON DESCRIBES HOW HE CARVED RICH PICKINGS, A FIVE FOOT MOUSE, AT LAST YEAR'S SCULPTREE EVENT

As you get older it appears time speeds up. No sooner had I finished one Sculptree event than the next one was upon me. I had a difficult time at the previous Sculptree because of my poor choice of timber, so this time I took care to choose a subject which would not need such a large piece, so I could hopefully use timber which was sound, rather than rotten to the core.

It is all very well having grandiose plans, but you soon realise a week (even using a chainsaw to speed up waste removal) is not very long. My decision to carve a mouse might seem staid compared to a stag leaping through the forest. But this was big tree carving, so why not make the mouse big, in fact why not a five foot mouse?

What a spectacle. It would certainly open the eyes of my cat! Could a mouse be that big? Yes, just take a large piece of oak (*Quercus spp.*), one Husqvarna chainsaw, a pinch of imagination, stir well for about a week and *Rich Pickings* can be created.

I called the piece *Rich Pickings* because this mouse had obviously found extremely rich pickings to grow to five feet, 1.5m. His nutritional success was also a slight handicap as his swollen belly gave him a little trouble in getting comfortable, hence the pose.

NATURAL DESIGN

The piece of oak I chose came from the base of the tree, so I had the root flare at the bottom to deal with. This made for subtle difficulties when planning the placing of the feet. But as the mouse had to have a base to stand safely, this area could be used to advantage. The trunk had a slight bend through it which was also incorporated into the design.

After looking at the timber I realised it was possible to use the whole piece and the natural shape to form the mouse. Most readers will be familiar with the conventional carving methods of blocking, arranging drawings of at least two sides on the block and sawing out from these guides to form a profile. So it may seem to some a rather dodgy way, in terms of accuracy, to start without this helping guide.

I could have used the traditional method but I would have had to reduce the whole carving in size, starting with a trunk some 30in, 76cm across the bottom, to some 28in, 71cm across its top. If I squared it off it would have measured only 20in, 51cm across if I was lucky.

You might feel happier doing it this way, but at times it can stop you from doing a piece simply because the material is not large enough to accommodate it. Much of the time, as my piece demonstrates, by studying the

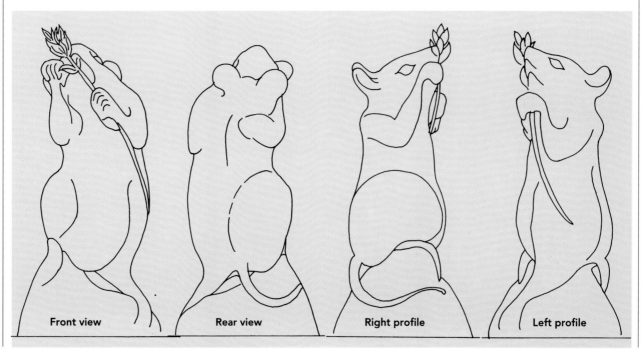

Front view   Rear view   Right profile   Left profile

material you can get what you want from it without squaring off the wood.

MARKING UP

I had measured and sketched the timber so I could make the drawing of the mouse fit the scale of the timber. It was then a simple but painstaking task translating various of the more prominent marks such as the outer lines, elbows, belly and hands onto the timber.

I measured from a fixed point (in a piece as tall as this I fixed a point from the base, but it could have been the top) with a simple set of lines through the vertical middle of the trunk on what I had chosen as the front, the rear and two sides. This gave a starting point to sketch in some of the outer lines that needed to be trimmed off to get the initial shape.

After I had made as many marks as I felt were necessary using my drawn plan,

....

With only a little sawing, I achieved a basic recognisable shape. Marks were picked up and redefined all around for the next stage of waste removal

I had only to freehand in the missing lines to give an outline. The lines can look quite odd on a rounded piece of timber compared to your drawing.

This is a point to watch. Don't be fooled into thinking just because your lines meet up completely, that after cutting round them you will be left with a perfect replica of your idea. If you are used to working with a square block, you can forget to compensate for the fact you are working with a round trunk while you are getting the drawing on to the wood.

This is really where you make or break the carving with either enough material left to shape correctly, or a distortion. And short of reducing the whole piece in size and starting again, your original idea may well be lost.

This particular example is a fairly easy shape but it can be complicated by arranging details first such as stance, to fit the timber. This is why it was useful to use the natural shape of the timber to see the mouse perched yet stretched, and reaching for his food.

I think this piece works all the way

round, but the front and back views please me the most, with the raised right leg and subtle twisting line starting from the base of the tail and running all the way up through the piece. Using the natural form of the log also meant all the movements matched the grain.

Where possible, after marking in the lines with a pen, chalk or crayon, I like to go over the marks with the chainsaw just to define them. I just run the tip of the saw over the line. I don't go any deeper than ½in, 13mm into the bark where the wood is to be saved, but go deeper where I am confident that any resulting chainsaw cuts can be carved away at a later stage.

This helps to define the lines, whereas pen or other markers can be a bit messy. The other benefit of this method of marking on round timber is that as you remove waste, some of the lines remain in place so you don't have to re-mark too much.

....

Below and below left **With a little more wood removed, all the major features were in place**

WASTE REMOVAL

When bandsawing round an outline from a square block you can often replace sawn sections for cutting outlines on the other plane. In round stock, the marks which remain can be joined up again and subsequently sawn along, taking you a step further to your finished position.

Once the major features have been transferred to the wood the plan becomes redundant. You can of course refer to your plans and models but it is a good idea to try and practice using

Left **Note the messy area in between the ears. The trick is not to go in too deeply with the chainsaw**

Below left **At this stage I was moving around the work, trimming, paring and defining details**

Below **I used gouges to help detail the smaller and finer features**

the semi-finished piece as a basis for visualising the finished work.

This imagination is surely what you started with to get the original idea, so why not keep using it to see in your mind what you are going to do next? Just like using a chisel to remove waste a little at a time, the saw can be used in the same way. You can chisel and define as you go depending on how you work, either all round or in sections. I prefer working in sections, gradually keeping all the areas together in their progression.

I carved the higher reaches of the piece from a scaffold, trying to keep the saw as low as possible. It was easier and less dangerous to work on the higher areas when working on a more level plane, and it also allowed a better view of the piece.

Below **Undercutting the belly and free leg**

At this stage especially, it is good practice to keep all your cutting as fine as possible. Some areas like between the ears were messy to do and difficult to cut with a chainsaw. I found the best way was not to go in too deep, and then tickle out the area with the saw.

DEFINITION

I was continuously moving around the work trimming and paring as well as marking and defining details like the claws and the ear of wheat. Then I continued with an Arbortech to begin the smoothing off. Next I used gouges to detail the smaller and finer wheat ears, teeth and claw areas. The main divisions were still done with the Arbortech as the scale allowed, but

Below **The whole thing was cleaned with light strokes from the Arbortech, and gouges used for inaccessible places**

cleaned with gouges.

The only major work left was at the base with the feet, lower legs and the base itself needing serious waste removal. I left this area until last to ensure the main aim of having the mouse configured in this pose worked. It would probably have been a mistake to set this area at the earlier stages and then model the mouse's upper body, leaving no room for refinement. I may not have got the perched yet stretched vision I wanted.

I increased the undercutting under the belly, under the free leg (where it had been cut through) and part of the tail until I was satisfied it looked right. This had to be balanced with the concern that too much undercutting would weaken the whole and risk a breakage.

I finally cleaned the whole thing with light strokes from the Arbortech, with the cutter honed to razor sharp. I used gouges for bits which were difficult to access such as the claws and teeth, leaving lovely contrasting patches of white sap wood around the claws, ears, tail and wheat. ●

Lee Dickenson has been a self-employed carver for nine years, undertaking a wide range of carving and sculptural commissions, architectural work, furniture and restoration. He now has work in private collections all over the UK, as well as in Europe, the USA and as far afield as India.

TO LIFE!

FEATURE

I met Leon Bronstein at the Art Multiple Exhibition at Dusseldorf, Germany. Bronstein's sculptures are collected by individuals and major corporations all over the world, from Argentina to South Africa but also in Italy, Germany and Japan.

Born in Moldavia, Russia, in 1951, he left for Israel aged 28. Soon after his arrival, at a time when he could not find employment, he was seduced by the beautiful grain of olive wood (*Olea spp.*).

In a small wood shop near the City of Caesarea, he carved his first figure since his childhood days. The small figure was so appealing, it launched his career as a sculptor and made him an overnight success, not only with tourists but also with Israel's avant garde.

His themes are universal. "I believe", he says, "all ideas come from life experiences which, since the days of Socrates and Aristotle, are innate. The effect of life experience on the

individual accounts for the heterogeneous society of mankind". His own life experience allows him to add innovative techniques to his impressive range of materials.

When Bronstein left the Soviet Union in 1979, his only condition was that his entire family be allowed to leave with him. The relationships between man and woman, mother and child, are recurring themes in his work because it is the source from which he draws strength, inspiration and his boundless optimism.

"Only when we feel secure in the knowledge of where we come from, can we feel confident and free-spirited about where we are going" he says. Much of his work radiates some of that knowledge, but above all his pursuit of spiritual freedom.

The spark of innocence, love and passion for freedom seems to transfer from his sculptures to the viewer, infecting him with that special brand of 'Bronstein optimism'.

He is adept at expressing physical and spiritual motion

He has a strong affinity with the great English sculptors of this century

Eva Masthoff meets Israeli sculptor Leon Bronstein, whose work celebrates life and liberty

as well as suggesting closeness and tenderness. Arms link, locked in a tender embrace or reach out. Heads are lowered in shared intimacy.

The daring stance of some of his sculptures defies gravity. That is where his training as an engineer and watchmaker come in handy, all that precision and immaculate planning.

Yet his treatment of his subjects is a response of the senses rather than the mind. In his world, the power and beauty of human relationship reigns supreme.

In his skilful hands, the human form undergoes a powerful transformation, and takes on a geometrical shape. His figures move delicately, stretch deliciously, surge upwards, beyond the confines of the wood.

In the semi-abstract figures he carves, Bronstein is aware he has a strong affinity with the great English sculptors of this century Henry Moore and Barbara Hepworth. However his environment, a studio at Caesarea, is quite unique. Leon

works in the open courtyard of a Citadel where he is exposed to the sun and sea breezes.

His work bench overlooks the ancient Herodian Harbour where the sound of the waves accompanies the sound of his work, and the jumble of foreign languages comes from the visitors as they walk around admiring his unique sculptures.

Leon says he finds olive wood very tricky to work with because in its original state it is gnarled and lined. Only a handful of sculptors rise to the challenge of using the natural grain in the wood. However, he continues chiselling slowly through its bark.

Usually his instinct tells him which parts of the wood should be removed. So once the natural grain reveals itself, Leon's skilful hands, the natural extension of his imagination and intellect, come up with another great piece of inspired art. He has a way of waking the latent images in the convoluted grain of olive wood. ●

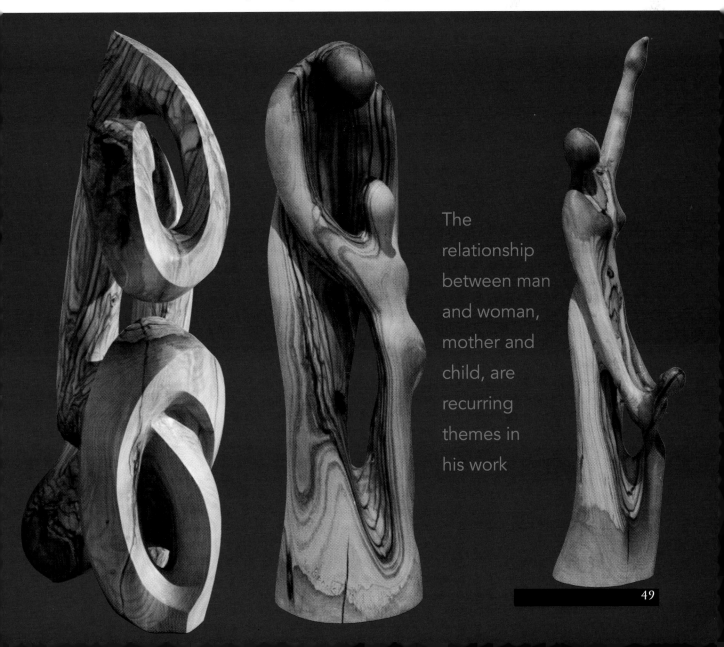

The relationship between man and woman, mother and child, are recurring themes in his work

49

THE WORLD IN HIS HANDS

Vic Wood profiles award-
winning Australian carver
Arnold Voll

Save the Earth in red
river gum (*Eucalyptus
camaldulensis*), one section
of tree. 2m x 900 x 800mm,
79 x 35½ x 31½in.

Arnold Voll, winner of numerous awards in sculpture and carving, is carrying on the influence of his grandfather who was an excellent carver. The catalyst for this started about 10 years ago when Arnold took an intensive woodturning course with me, and this is where he learnt the basic knowledge of wood. From there he ventured towards carving and sculpture.

While working in the business of decorative art and party cooking, his nature was always to hurry. Nothing could wait. But since retiring eight years ago Arnold has been surprised at the change of pace, and the reward of being patient. When he gets into carving and sculpture the world is altogether forgotten.

Therapy

The use of wood is appropriate for what Arnold is doing. He says, "It is like therapy when I create an object. Without the creation of forms, my life would be empty. I don't think I would be this fit and mentally balanced. It is truly a fulfilling occupation and can be recommended to all."

One challenging experience Arnold had when collecting firewood was when he came across a huge tree fork which had recently fallen in a storm. He could visualise a man and a woman with the globe of the world above their heads.

Wood gathering came to a halt, and using his four wheel drive truck and a winch he was able to manoeuvre it onto a trailer and home.

After roughing out the two figures and the globe, Arnold drilled every limb through the centre with a 20mm, ¾in auger, enabling the wood on the limbs and body to dry from within.

Top heavy

When this had been done he realised the globe made the sculpture top heavy. There was no alternative. He cut the globe off at the hands, then cut the globe in half with a hand saw and hollowed it out with an Arbortech, glued it back together and replaced it back on the hands, with the joining line acting as the equator.

This piece of work took two Australian hot summers to dry. The figures were coated with Mobil car or end coat sealer.

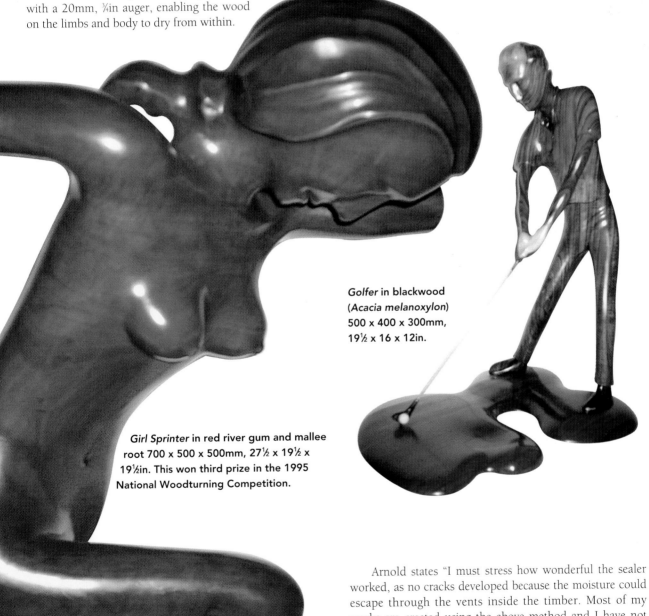

Golfer in blackwood
(*Acacia melanoxylon*)
500 x 400 x 300mm,
19½ x 16 x 12in.

Girl Sprinter in red river gum and mallee root 700 x 500 x 500mm, 27½ x 19½ x 19½in. This won third prize in the 1995 National Woodturning Competition.

Arnold states "I must stress how wonderful the sealer worked, as no cracks developed because the moisture could escape through the vents inside the timber. Most of my works are created using the above method and I have not lost one through cracking."

The piece was finished with three coats of acrylic lacquer.

Arnold really loves working with wood, removing each unwanted piece. He always works well into the night, and then cannot wait to continue

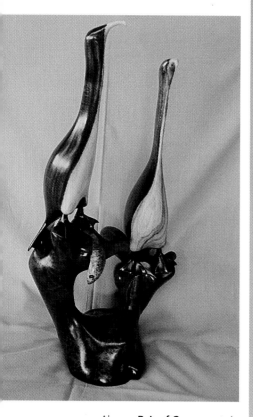

Above **Pair of Cormorants** in blackwood 450 x 450 x 350mm, 17¾ x 17¾ x 14in. This piece won the Bega Woodcrafters Sculpture and Carving section.
Right **Egret** in jarrah burl (*Eucalyptus marginata*), mallee root and red river gum 700 x 700 x 700mm, 27½ x 27½ x 27½in. This won the Victorian Woodworkers Association Carving and Sculpture section and the National Woodwork Competition Sculpture section.
Below right **John the Baptist**, a commission in huon pine (*Dacrydium franklinii*) 850 x 650 x 60mm, 33½ x 25½ x 2⅜in.

his work the next morning.

This feeling is portrayed in the work while there is a desire for it, or until the idea expires.

There is a strong sense of movement in Arnold's work, and this is often enhanced by his choice of material and use of colour.

He portrays in his carvings and sculptures an opportunity for the viewer to receive some of the vibes of the maker, for example in *Pair of Cormorants* and *The Double Statue*. ●

Arnold Voll
R.M.B. 4090
Mansfield 3732
Victoria
Australia.

THE LIZARD OF OZ

JOHN NOTTAGE SHOWS HOW TO CARVE SOME FIERCE LOOKING AUSTRALIAN ANIMALS

In issue 34 (March/April) I told of the inspiration behind my carvings of Australian wildlife, and showed some of my circle of life carvings.

In this issue I will show how to carve three animals that live in remote and arid areas of the outback, a shingle back lizard, a knob tail gecko and a juvenile bilby.

I have selected these three from the vast range of Australian wildlife. Indeed, deciding what to carve is the first big decision you have to make, because in the world of nature the list is endless.

The next thing you need to decide is the pose or posture of the animal. For example, a carving of a snake is far more exciting if you show it coiled with head back ready to strike, rather than stretched out in a straight line.

Having chosen an animal it is vital to study its form. Decide on a posture which would best represent the animal in a lifelike and exciting way.

Try to study the animal in the wild or in a zoo if possible, but if not look in libraries for books and magazines. Work from photographs, not drawings or paintings.

The shingle back lizard is a member of the skink family. I carved it with a curve to its body, its head raised, mouth open and tongue out because the lizard adopts this posture when in danger to give itself a threatening appearance.

It has strong jaws and could give a nasty bite, though it is generally harmless, living on snails, plants and berries.

TEMPLATE

First draw and cut out a cardboard template. This lizard has four legs in different positions, so it is best to make the template as if looking directly down from above.

For this project I used jelutong (*Dyera costulata*), an excellent carving wood from South East Asia, which takes on a bronzed look when finely sanded.

Another wood I use when painting the wood is radiata pine (*Pinus radiata*). This is not good for carving, and the right grain structure has to be picked out, but it is a building material in plentiful supply and cheaper than most carving woods, of which there are many in Australia.

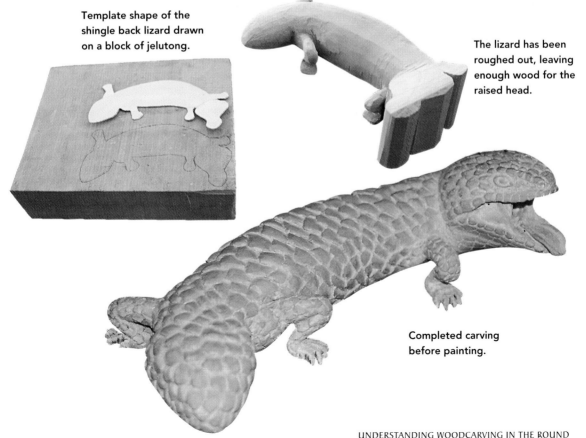

Template shape of the shingle back lizard drawn on a block of jelutong.

The lizard has been roughed out, leaving enough wood for the raised head.

Completed carving before painting.

The completed lizard in its natural habitat.

....

I used a block of wood 80mm, 3⅛in thick. The thicker the wood the more you can raise the lizard's head.

Unfortunately I have found it difficult to buy blocks of jelutong more than about 75mm, 3in thick, so if I need a larger block I have to laminate pieces together.

I cut the template outline out on my 355mm, 14in bandsaw, cutting outside the line to allow some spare wood. Cutting out wood this thick is not easy, so take your time.

You cannot cut out this thickness of shape with a scroll or fret saw, so think about and plan each cut in advance.

With the top view cut out, think about the side view. Draw this on the wood and cut it out.

Draw a centre line down the rough sawn block and keep re-drawing it whenever you carve it away, as this helps maintain symmetry.

When carving I use whatever tools will get the job done, chainsaws, Arbortech, Powerfile, Dremel, chisels and knives. I will even make my own tools if I need to for a particular job. Always use a good dust mask or respirator when using power tools.

When carving an animal I sometimes start from the head and work down, and sometimes carve from the bottom up. Sometimes it just goes in one even flow, I just work instinctively. With this lizard I worked from the tail up to the head.

HEAD

Bearing in mind I had to allow for carving shingle-like scales, I took the bulk of the waste off with a Powerfile.

I next used the Dremel to rough out the legs and to work up the body to the head. I used a short drill bit in the Dremel.

I carved the top half of the head first, then worked out where the bottom jaw would go and cut away

waste from underneath that.

Mark the position of the eyes and carve them in. The eyes are often the most important part of the animal as they convey its character: fierceness, timidity, fear, aggression and so on.

Finish the head by carving the inner mouth.

The lizard has five toes, so leave those until last, together with the shingle-like scales.

Sand the carving with 80 to 150 grit abrasive paper. To reach awkward places you can stick some abrasive on to some scrap sticks of the right shape to make mini sanding rasps.

I decided to paint this lizard as the animal has a bright colour scheme, and so colour makes it more life-like.

Before painting brush the carving with two coats of water-based wood adhesive mixed 50–50 with water, allowing it to dry between coats.

This seals the wood and prevents the paint running or showing darker on different hardnesses of grain.

GECKO

The knob tailed gecko is a small lizard-type animal with a large head and big eyes which give it facial expressions of greater character than most reptiles.

It has skinny legs and a robust body, and when threatened it arches its back like a cat and makes angry hissing noises, so this was the pose I decided to carve it in.

The template, jelutong blank and sawn out shape for the knob tail gecko.

The gecko before painting.

I decided to carve the head first and worked out the position of the eyes and other facial features before carving them in with the Dremel and a small drill bit.

The finished gecko in its natural habitat.

I also used a home-made rasp, some knives and abrasive paper.

Carve the body details next, followed by the tail and finally the legs and toes.

Seal the animal as mentioned previously before painting.

This time draw the template with a side view and cut the shape out with a scroll saw from a small piece of jelutong.

The body is about 90mm, 3½in long, but with the tail it comes to 125mm, 5in long x 50mm, 2in wide.

When rough shaping the body make it slightly oversize to allow for later adjustments.

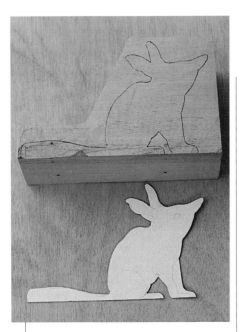

Left **The template and white cheesewood blank for the bilby.**

Left **The carved bilby before painting.**

Below **The finished bilby in its natural habitat.**

BILBY

The bilby is about the size of a rabbit when full grown and is now quite rare in the wild in Australia having been widely hunted for its fur.

It has also been the victim of predators such as the fox and cat, and rabbits and farm livestock destroying its habitat.

It is related to the bandicoot, has excellent sense of hearing and smell, and digs burrows 2m, 6ft 7in deep. It eats plants, roots and insects.

Juvenile bilbys are cute little creatures, and I decided to carve the animal in an alert, sitting up pose.

Cut out a side view template, bearing in mind the template is only a guide to the shape and basic dimensions, so make it slightly oversize as usual.

For this carving I used a 125mm, 5in thick block of white cheesewood (*Wrighta laeuis mullgar*), a native Australian wood.

Cut the profile view out on the bandsaw, and mark a centreline on the blank before roughing out, as before.

Start with the head, carving out the eyes, ears and snout, before moving down to the body, legs, feet and lastly the tail.

After carving in the details sand and seal the work as before prior to painting.●

Arbortech available in the UK from
BriMarc Associates,
8 Ladbroke Park, Millers Road,
Warwick CV34 5AE.
Tel: 01926 493389.

Powerfile available in the UK from
Black & Decker Ltd,
210 Bath Road,
Slough, Berkshire SL1 3YD.
Tel: 01753 511234.

Dremel available in the UK from
Robert Bosch Ltd,
PO Box 98, Broadwater Park,
North Orbital Road, Denham,
Uxbridge, Middlesex UB9 5HJ.
Tel: 01895 834466.

John Nottage was born in West Cliff, Essex in 1949 but moved to Australia aged two when his parents emigrated. He worked in the earth moving industry for most of his life and had his own business for 12 years. He has worked around Australia including in an iron ore mine. He currently lives in Luddenham, NSW, and his interests include astronomy and keeping parrots.

MARCHING TO A DIFFERENT DRUM

Former army chaplain James Thompson talks to Ann and Bob Phillips about his new career as a wildlife carver

From Major in the United States army to full-time wildlife carver was quite a career jump for Jim Thompson. He pursued his first career as a military chaplain-counsellor in the US and abroad, including a stint as combat chaplain in the Vietnam war. Well established in the hierarchy for fifteen years, he was set for a secure progression through the system. Then he gave it all up.

Jim Thompson in his days as a combat chaplain in the US army

Research is essential: here a paper pattern for a ring neck pheasant is developed from photographs

Bald eagle feeding on rainbow trout

The change came with an introduction to master carver, Roscoe Condon. This meeting, and subsequent instruction in woodcarving from Roscoe, rekindled Jim's boyhood interest in natural history. He had grown up in rural areas, and enjoyed hunting and fishing. Starting to carve initially as a hobby, in less than a year Jim had sold his first carving and received the first of many major awards, setting him on the path to a second career.

Watching brief

Jim's approach to carving is essentially a realistic one. As he puts it: 'You have to know what you're carving before you carve it.' To this end he spends time observing live birds and maintains a large and constantly expanding reference library of ornithological books, journals, pictures and slides.

Jim spends time observing live birds and maintains a large and constantly expanding reference library

 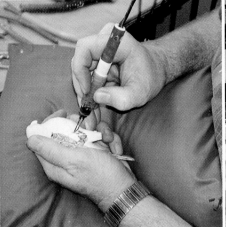 

Above from left to right

Basswood roughed out on the bandsaw

Detailed texturing with a pyrography tool

Painting a quail with a study skin to ensure absolute accuracy

This advance study saves him from the embarrassing errors committed by more 'ornithologically naïve' carvers. For example, a sculpture of a bald eagle attacking a rabbit looks very dramatic; but, as Jim points out, their prairie habitat just doesn't supply rabbits. Even worse, he cites the carving of a rare bird species with a curious hump on its back. The artist had copied a picture without realising that the bird was part of a population study and so had a transmitter strapped to its back!

Artistic interpretation

Accuracy isn't all that's needed, however. Realism in Jim's terms means 'detail without feather-counting'. The carving has to have life: he aims to create a sculpture that is immediately recognisable yet artistically conceived in both design and composition.

He believes the display setting and pose for a bird carving also need to be aesthetically pleasing, but based on knowledge of what is appropriate. Posing a Harris hawk on a cactus is

Miniature banded dotterel, a member of the plover family

Silver eye finch

fine, for example, but for a bald eagle it's not such a good idea.

Depending on the species, the carvings may be full size or anything from one-fifth to three-quarters life size. Full-size sculptures are stunning but not everyone has the income, not to mention the space for, say, the 110in, 2800 mm wingspan of a carved condor. Songbirds and other small birds are usually carved life size, but pheasants, geese and many waterfowl are produced to scale.

Working methods

In either case his work pattern is similar. After studying the subject, Jim develops a pattern for the bird in the pose he requires. This two-dimensional pattern is developed into a three-dimensional model. First the pattern blank is cut out on a bandsaw, and then hand carved.

It's important to orient the grain to ensure any areas of stress are strong enough; to do this it may be necessary to laminate several pieces together.

A limited range of woods is used, since in most cases the grain will be obscured by paint. Stylised birds such as the eagle look stunning in American black walnut (*Juglans niger*), but for birds that are to be painted, basswood (American

lime, *Tilia americana*) is the timber of choice.

Tools used are knives and hand-held power tools. Jim is an ardent advocate of sharp knives: 'You don't cut yourself with the sharp tools... it's the blunt blades that are the culprits. Sharp knives are easier to guide and control with less pressure.'

You don't cut yourself with the sharp tools… it's the blunt blades that are the culprits. Sharp knives are easier to control

However, he can recall one occasion when sharp knives caused him injury. Tossing a newly purchased set of knives in his car one day, he nonchalantly leapt into his seat to find the package had caught in the seat cushion, offering up the point to his behind. As Jim has it, showing his well-known fondness for puns: 'I really got the point, even if it made me the butt of my students' jokes.' Freak accidents and anecdotes aside though, sharp tools are normally desirable and safest.

Miniature finch

Racing pigeon

Finishing touches

After the carving has been completed, Jim uses a pyrography tool for fine feather texturing. He paints with acrylics, working closely from a model or a detailed photograph for reference. To display the bird in a suitable habitat Jim sculpts leaves, rocks and plants in either wood or metal.

Often a degree of experimentation is called for: would cactus spikes, for example, be better made from wood or steel? And should the work then be encased in glass for customer safety?

Jim's realistic yet sensitive approach to his carving compositions gives his pieces wide appeal, and his collectors now range from country and western stars to financiers. He is a man of many parts: committed chaplain, experienced counsellor, wonderful carver ... and a truly appalling punster.

His students clearly enjoy their courses, even if Jim's irrepressible humour means that they need to have sharp wits as well as sharp carving tools. Those relentless puns are integral to the lessons. Or, as Jim would have it: 'Carving gives me the chance to be a full-time cut-up (joker) and get away with it!' ∎

Ann and Bob Phillips are professional woodworkers, based in New Zealand. Coming from backgrounds in science and engineering they apply the same high standards to their creative work; in 1994 they were awarded a New Zealand government quality award. They have written widely on woodworking and their book *Make Money from Woodturning* is published by GMC Publications

Jim today, with his earliest attempts at carving

Life-size falcon

PROJECT

PUFFIN AWAY

A STEP BY STEP GUIDE BY ROGER SCHROEDER TO CARVING ONE OF THESE DISTINCTIVE BIRDS

Puffins are members of the auk family, and there are several different species. I chose to carve the Atlantic or common puffin using American black walnut (*Juglans nigra*), as it is predominantly black.

Puffins are almost comical in the way they jump around and seem to be in such a hurry when on land. So I decided to give this one an animated pose. Two things contributed to that. One was turning the head so that it was perpendicular to the forward thrust of the body. A turned or upturned head is something I incorporate into nearly all my bird carvings. The other was having the bird walking down a sloping rock surface, which suggested a pedestal of sorts.

Common puffin (*Fratercula artica*) in American black walnut, by Roger Schroeder. Winner of the First in Show prize for an interpretive sculpture at the World Championship Wildfowl Carving Competition in Maryland, USA

PATTERNS AND PROFILES

I spent some time drawing my patterns, a side and front view. They were critical because I had chosen a walnut log measuring only 10in, 250mm in diameter. But the wood was well seasoned and stable, and seemed free of defects.

To bandsaw the profiles I had to flatten the log a bit. This meant doing one profile, gluing the waste back on to the profile with a few spots of hot-melt glue, and then cutting out the other profile. What was left was a Picasso-inspired shape ready for rounding and detailing. Extra wood was left on the flanks so I could position the raised primary feathers.

The bandsawn block was bolted to a piece of scrap wood which held it in place in my bench vice. Carving began with rounding the body. For much of the bulk removal of wood I used a

Bandsawn profile, ready to be carved

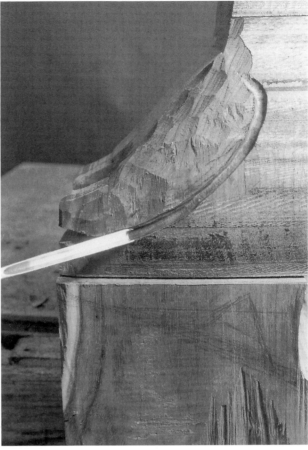

Above left **Fishtail gouges were used to round the body, taking careful note of the grain direction so as not to remove too much wood**

Above right **A narrow 7mm fluter gouge is perfect for defining boundaries, here between the wings and the body**

Below **Power carver with a needle-shaped tungsten carbide rasp removes the parts other tools cannot reach**

Swiss-made No.3 35mm fishtail gouge. I took great care with the direction of the grain so that I did not break out large chunks of wood.

A No.9 15mm gouge was used to take away wood where the neck meets the body. Then to define where the wings fold against the body I used a No.11 7mm fluter gouge, which is perfect for mapping out territories or defining boundaries where areas are to be relieved.

POWER PLUS

I enjoy using power tools for shaping, refining and sanding. Here a carbide file cutter in the handpiece of a flexible-shaft angle-grinder was used to smooth away the facets made by the hand tools.

Wood was removed on the body, leaving the wings raised, with a No.5 20mm gouge. For sharper definitions, for example marking the pitch of the rock on which the bird is standing, I used a Swiss No.14 12mm v-tool with a rounded apex.

To keep some order to the wood removal, I started taking wood away from between the legs of the bird with a No.11 7mm fluter and a No.9 15mm gouge. Another power tool I use is the Dremel Moto-Tool power carver: with a small needle-shaped tungsten carbide rasp I was able to remove wood between the legs that would be difficult to reach with traditional carving tools.

DESIGN DILEMMA

An important consideration when designing this piece was how much to separate the bird from the rock. I didn't want to push the wood to its limits so

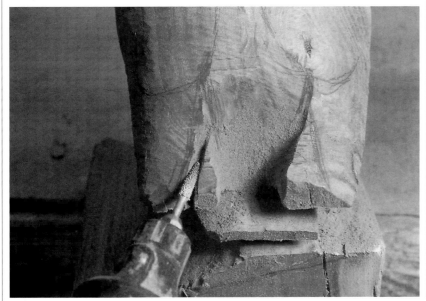

that it would be fragile, nor did I want the bird to appear to be emerging from the rock. My decision was to undercut the wood enough, using the No.14 12mm v-tool, so that it would look as though the bird was walking forward, although it was in fact sitting on the rock. The illusion seems to,work.

After removing wood from under the body, the rump had to be rounded with a No.5 12mm gouge. Again the Moto-tool was used with a tungsten carbide rasp to take away wood from under the rump and tail, and with a serrated knife-edged cutter to smooth the surface.

Removing wood from between the primary feathers and the tail had to be done with great care because the grain runs vertically through the primary feathers. Here I used a Swiss No.12 8mm v-tool, and then the Moto-tool to remove more wood from the protruding primaries. It was particularly useful here to avoid pounding away at such fragile areas. To me this is the best of what power carving can achieve when it comes to detailing.

I find it helpful to draw in centre-lines for guidance when I'm carving. At this point I drew the centreline for the body, then worked away from either side of the line with a No.5 20mm gouge, and smoothed the wood with the carbide cutter.

FEET FIRST

Next I turned to the feet. These birds have webbed feet with sharp claws ideally suited for digging nesting holes;

Top **The body, undercut with a v-tool to create the illusion that the bird is separate from the rock**

Centre **The grain runs vertically through the primary feathers, so work here has to be careful. A power carver refines work done with a v-tool**

Right **Having drawn on and outlined the foot with a power carver and rasp, it is relieved with a gouge**

the inner toes and claws are twisted sideways. Once I decided on the position of the forward foot, I flattened out the area with the No.5 20mm gouge and the carbide file cutter. I drew the foot on the wood and defined its outline with the Moto-Tool and tungsten carbide rasp, then relieved the foot with a No.5 12mm gouge.

Using a 60°, 8mm v-tool, I removed wood from under the belly of the bird. The other foot is partially hidden under the belly. I took my time laying it out, making sure it had the same dimensions as the protruding foot.

I like the idea of showing well-defined parts of the anatomy as points of interest on a carving, so I decided to emphasise the claws with a needle-shaped burr on the power carver, which cut the wood quickly and accurately.

A tricky manoeuvre was defining the rear of the partially concealed foot. To do this I had to remove more wood from behind the protruding leg and used my tungsten-carbide rasp in the Moto-Tool.

HEAD LINES

With the body shaped, but not sanded, I went to work on the head. Puffin heads are fascinating because of their distinctive parrot-like beaks. Here, using a centreline, I drew on the top profile of the head, and the details of the beak and eyes.

To define the beak I used the 7mm fluter gouge. In this area it was advan-

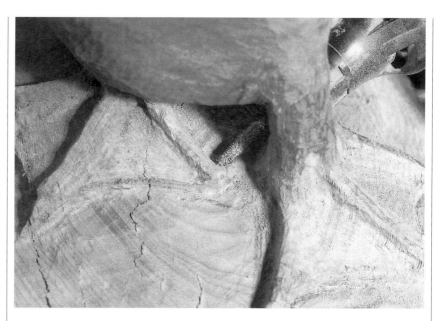

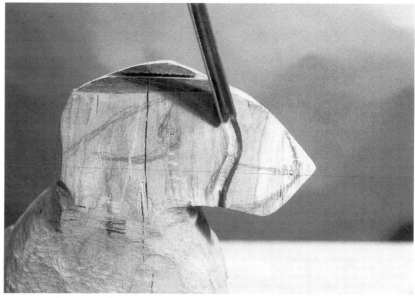

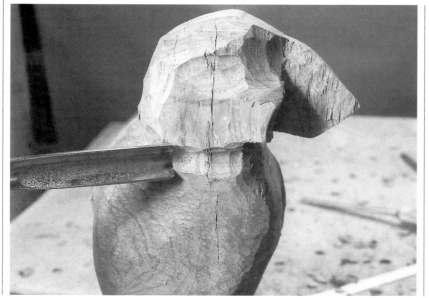

Top **A tricky manoeuvre, defining the rear of the partially concealed back foot**

Centre **Details are drawn on the head and defined. The beak has been left deliberately long to allow for shaping**

Left **The head takes shape, with eye channels, a more rounded profile and clearer separation from the body**

tageous that the grain ran up and down. I had left the beak longer than it needed to be as I had no intention of adding on wood. In the event I was a bit over-zealous when carving the tip: I worked gingerly, only taking slivers of wood away, but I used a No.7 20mm gouge, which may have been oversized for the purpose.

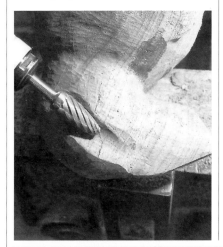

Next I rounded the head and defined what might be called eye channels, using a No.9 15mm gouge. At this stage the puffin was still very 'cheeky' and oversized, but the anatomy had taken shape.

Using the No.9 15mm gouge, I removed more wood from around the neck area. The carbide burr in the flexible shaft angle-grinder was excellent for helping to shape the beak, and making indentations on the face.

The whole body was sanded with a ¾in, 20mm diameter cushioned drum sander. This accepts various grit

Left **Refining the contours with a flexible-shaft machine**

Below **Callipers used to position the eyes symmetrically**

Bottom **Power sanding smooths wood around the detailed eye area**

sandpaper, but cloth-backed paper works best because it does not tear easily.

EYE TO EYE

Going back to the head, I drew in the separation of the upper and lower mandibles, and the fleshy skin where they meet. I wanted the head to be a major focal point and felt that putting in some details would do the trick. Symmetry was important here.

Callipers were useful for locating the exact position of the eyes on either side of the head. Relieving the eyes was done with the 8mm v-tool, and a small gouge, and it was sanded with a ¼in, 6mm diameter cartridge roll of sandpaper on a mandrel that fitted into my flexible shaft handpiece.

The 60° 8mm v-tool was used to mark off the beak from the face and to separate the upper and lower mandibles.

FINE FINISH

To finish the puffin, I went to finer and finer cloth-backed sandpaper, using rotary tools and sanding by hand to get it smooth. This was followed by two coats of Deft brushing lacquer – a semi-gloss finish. This dries quickly, usually within half an hour, and it buffs out with steel wool to leave a smooth surface. From there it was off to the competitions! ●

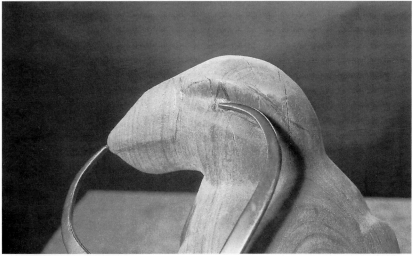

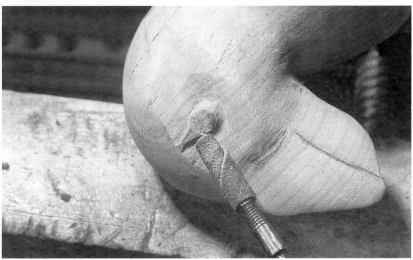

Roger Schroeder is a prolific writer and lecturer on woodworking, construction, sculpture and carving, as well as a cabinetmaker and amateur carver. He combines these activities with a full-time job as a high school English teacher, specialising in teaching creative writing and research

DECORATIVE DUPLICATE

ROD NAYLOR EXPLAINS HOW HE COPIED A RESIN CASTING OF A DANCING FIGURE INTO EBONY

The inspiration for the *Deco Dancer* was a cheap, broken polyester resin casting. Although the basic idea was good, I didn't like the finer points. The overall line was not very fluid and any detail which did exist was crude.

My solution was to re-glue the pieces, and partially coat the original with a layer of epoxy resin. This had the advantage of a slow setting time, during which it could be manipulated like a piece of clay. After hardening, the whole sculpture was re-carved using ordinary tools.

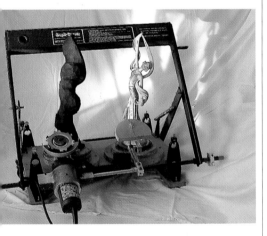

The Dupli-Carver with angle grinder and Arbortech

The final ebony (*Diospyrus spp*) carving was copied from the resin. As a professional carver, I find using traditional pointing methods too slow to be profitable. When you produce a carving, you are judged on the merits of the end product, not on the way it was achieved. So I believe anything which may enhance the result is legitimate. My solution was to use a Dupli-Carver copier.

First, I glued and screwed the resin onto a piece of scrap board which was then screwed onto a turntable. Then I glued and screwed a roughly rectangular block of ebony, about 6mm, 1 ¼in larger than the pattern, onto another turntable. I placed an extra piece of scrap underneath, as I didn't want to copy the base of the pattern.

Both turntables were then fitted onto the Dupli-Carver. These copying jigs work on the principle of a three-dimensional pantograph. Any movement made by a stylus is repeated by a high speed cutter. As the stylus is moved over the pattern, the cutter repeats every movement, passing through any material which gets in the way.

ROUGH CUTS

I did the initial roughing out by fitting an angle grinder and Arbortech into the jig. First, I fitted a dummy disc or stylus, slightly bigger than the real cutter. This was because I wanted to leave a generous 3mm, ⅛in above the final surface before carving in the detail.

The advantage of an angle grinder rather than a router is speed. Depending on the type of disc selected, it can give up to 100,000 more cuts per minute than a router.

With the stylus set 6mm, ¼in too far out, I completed the preliminary roughing out in minutes. The shape was achieved without any need for measurements or calculations. A second cut was then taken with

Rear view of the *Deco Dancer* 390 x 100 x 70 mm, 15¼ x 4 x 2¾ in with Scagliola base.

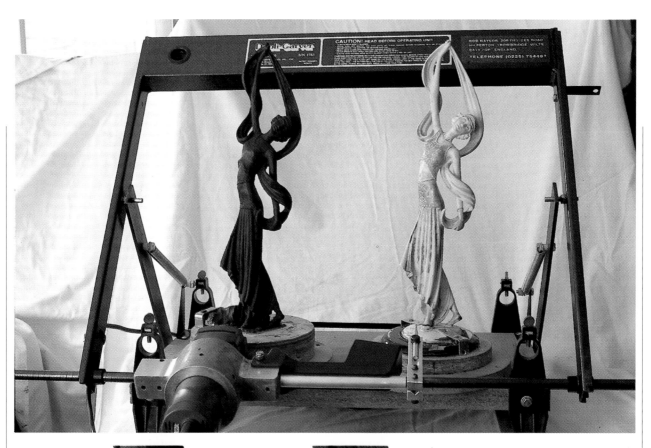

Above **The Dupli-Carver with router**
Left **Detail carved by the Dupli-Carver**

the stylus set 3mm, ⅛in too far out. This left the finished carving, hidden by a 3mm, ⅛in skin of ebony.

Roughing out to this stage took about one hour, but the main disadvantage of carving with a 100mm, 4in diameter cutting disc is you cannot follow fine detail.

Alternatives to roughing out by this method are:

1 Make accurate templates and bandsaw to shape. This method is still relatively crude.
2 Fit a long thin bit into a router in the copying jig. Put a stylus against each of the prominent features on the pattern to drill a corresponding hole in the wood. A cutting disc could then be used to cut away the wood freehand until the holes started to vanish.
3 Fit a Tornado cutter into a router in the copying jig.

The Tornado is a smaller version of the Arbortech and fits into a router, die grinder or flexible drive shaft. It is less efficient than the Arbortech for

bulk removal, but has the advantage of being able to cut finer detail and does not require an angle grinder.

My next step was to exchange the angle grinder in the Dupli-Carver for a router. Although a square-ended cutter will remove wood quickly, I prefer a round-ended one. A square end, being more aggressive, would cause vibration and distortion as the slender figure would flex.

I used a 12.5mm, ½in diameter cutter with a 19mm, ¾in stylus. Like the 100mm, 4in diameter cutting disc I used previously, this left a 3mm, ⅛in skin above the finished surface. But it reached into the larger hollows which the cutting disc could not.

Starting on the high spots and working back into the hollows and from the top to the bottom, I rotated the turntables while carving to reach right around the figure. I ignored detail below the bottom of the dress, as this section was needed to keep the block of wood stable while carving.

DECORATIVE DETAIL

The basic shape was now starting to appear, but the 19mm, ¾in stylus could not reach into the detail. I kept the 12.5mm ½in cutter but used a matching stylus next, so the carving machine now copied exactly.

At this stage I stopped rotating the carving, until I had also used the finer cutters and styli. These were able to carve in the smaller detail.

After one area was complete to the bottom of the dress, I partially rotated the carving and then started again with the larger cutters and styli, this being the most precise method for detailed work.

When the carving had been rotated right round, it was complete except for the feet. To do these meant removing some of the metal brackets which were largely responsible for holding the ebony down.

I started roughing out again. But as the figure was held more loosely with some brackets and a bead of hot melt glue, I used a 3mm, ⅛in diameter round-ended cutter with a 6mm, ¼in stylus. When the feet had been roughed out in this way, I changed the stylus to one which matched the cutter, enabling work on the carving machine to be finished.

Total carving time up to this point was 12 hours. This included all stages from cutting out the block to finishing detail, such as fingers, eyes and even eyebrows. I smoothed out the small ripples left by the router using a variety of techniques:

1 I used a file to smooth convex areas.
2 I used fine tungsten carbide or diamond burrs with a flexible drive machine and rotary handpiece to smooth deep hollows.

I also used tungsten carbide and diamond burrs with a reciprocating handpiece. The rapid vibrating action gave a more controllable action than was possible with a rotary movement. Reciprocating handpieces are designed to be used with chisels. To use them with a filing action you need to fit a spring, or tape an elastic band around the floating head, to keep it pressed against the cam.

3 I used chisels, gouges and knives to reach into some hollows and corners.

The ebony accepted minute detail, right down to fingernails and hair. On the negative side, it showed up every flaw, even 500 grit paper did not leave a polished surface. I carried out final smoothing with charcoal, and then charcoal mixed with micro-crystalline wax. Not only did this impart a soft sheen, but it left black deposits in the hollows, rather than the white normally left by wax. ●

Above **Filing smooth the convex areas**
Left **Detail of the *Deco Dancer***

The Dupli-Carver is available from Rod Naylor at 208 Devizes Road, Hilperton, Trowbridge, Wilts BA14 7QP
Tel: 01225 754497

Rod Naylor is primarily a woodcarver who works in a variety of styles from traditional to modern. His work is in public and private collections around the world.
As well as working as a restorer for museums and the National Trust, and as a consultant for collectors, publishers and tool companies, Rod also produces work for other carvers and designs and makes carving equipment.

BIRD IN A BOX

TERRY EVERITT SHOWS HOW HE MAKES ATTRACTIVE NATUREBOXES FEATURING CARVED BRITISH BIRDS

Below **Top and side view drawings of the grey wagtail.**

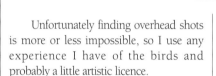

This *Naturebox* is my contribution to the world of wildlife art. It has developed over a six-month period, and originated as an alternative to my paintings of British birds.

I have to admit I am not really a woodcarver but a wildlife artist who has exchanged brushes, paper and paint for wood, knives, files and a dart.

My aim is to portray in wood some of our most attractive British birds in a creative and artistic setting.

SKETCHES

As with all projects, I start off with a few rough sketches of the bird I intend to carve, usually in the pose I feel will look best for that particular species. For this project I carved a grey wagtail.

Once I have decided on the most favourable sketch I draw the bird again from a side view and an overhead view, using as much reference as possible to get as much detail as I can to make the bird realistic.

A selection of completed *Natureboxes*.

Unfortunately finding overhead shots is more or less impossible, so I use any experience I have of the birds and probably a little artistic licence.

Once the sketches are completed I select a suitable piece of English lime (*Tilia vulgaris*) from my stock of off-cuts. After checking the material for splits or damage I transfer the drawings onto the side and top of the wood using a piece of rouge paper or tracing down paper, which can be bought at art supplies shops.

To ensure I have good clean lines for the first cuts I always go over the outline with a sharp pencil to make sure I can see where the lines are when working on my bandsaw.

CUTTING OUT

I have a small Burgess Mk II bandsaw which does not cope well with timber 50mm, 2in thick, but it is still quicker than cutting by hand. It was a gift, so the screeching is well worth putting up with.

The next step is to take away as much material as possible, and at this point the bird is cut minus his beak and legs which are made separately.

Once the final cuts are made I again redraw the bird's side view and top view, this time by hand using my original drawings as reference.

I ensure I am happy with the layouts before starting to carve, and if not, use an ordinary rubber to erase and start again.

I draw in a centre line down the bird to help in carving the bird symmetrically.

CARVING

I am not sure whether I should describe myself as a woodcarver, whittler or a wood butcher, as chisels are not part of my tool kit.

I started this venture while unemployed, so I basically used tools I already had, saving precious cash on tools I just could not afford.

My extensive range of carving tools comprises one craft knife, three scalpels with different shaped blades, two needle files, one flat and one round, and a dart.

The carving of the bird is a tense time for my wife Sarah, who waits with sticking plasters in hand for the first slip with the knife.

As the song goes, The First Cut is the Deepest. This is true, as after the first cut I tend to be a tad more careful and normally end up with just half a dozen small nicks.

This is one of the pitfalls of using only knives and always carving with the workpiece in my hand. So be warned, those fingerless mitts could be a perfect fit if you don't take care.

My intention when carving is to take off as much bulk as possible with the craft knife, and then when I get nearer to my finished size I use one of my scalpels to gradually whittle away the wood.

In this way I do not take away too much, as it's difficult to replace any huge divot chopped out by being over enthusiastic.

During the carving I always refer to my drawings, and sketch on the workpiece where the wings start and finish, and any other lines I need to work to.

I find the most important points at this stage are keeping check on all my reference books and looking at the carving from every angle for shape and symmetry until I am happy with it.

Once I have managed to get down to the correct size and shape I clean up with my files and use a piece of flour paper to finish off.

As you can see from the photographs, these birds are not polished when completed, but I like a clean, smooth surface for cutting in the wing and tail feathers.

Once again all relevant details are drawn onto the bird and checked against drawings and reference books to ensure they are correct before starting work.

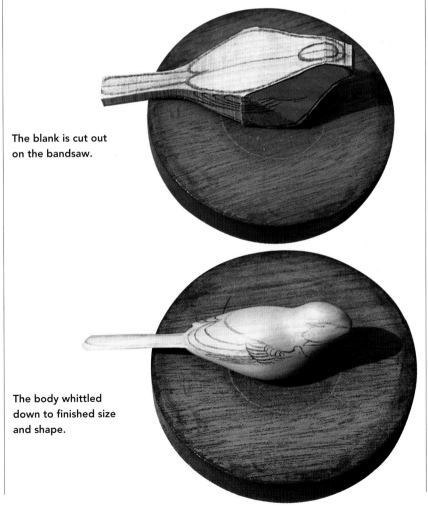

The blank is cut out on the bandsaw.

The body whittled down to finished size and shape.

This is where my scalpel, with a nicely pointed No 11 blade, comes into its own.

The most accurate and crucial work now has to be done in the carving of the wing feathers, and at this point I concentrate hard, knowing any slips mean it's back to square one.

TEXTURING

With the detail work carved in, it's on to texturing.

Being unemployed, my first hurdle was I could not afford a pyrography tool for texturing, used by most woodcarvers for this job.

As the carvings I produce are fairly small I needed to find something small enough to do the job but large enough to hold and control comfortably.

This is where the darts come in. The points on darts are hardened, so I found them perfect for the job. They have a fine point, a barrel the size of a pencil, and are easy to sharpen on a piece of wet and dry abrasive paper or stone.

I put texturing into two categories, the body feathers and wing and tail feathers. The dart is used only for the body feathers, where it is safe to put adequate pressure on to leave the correct amount of detail.

The short strokes are carried out by more or less following the contour of the bird's body making sure the point is quickly moved through the wood.

The wings have been carved, texturing completed and the beak fitted.

If it is dragged through slowly you will find little furry bits appearing on the surface and it is possible to end up with a robin dressed in an angora jumpsuit.

Wing feathers have to be treated with a little more delicacy as it is easy to break up the finely carved edges, so the dart goes back into it's case.

I have found a sharp knife blade is not an ideal tool either because it tends to cut through the wood rather than leave a visible indentation.

Thank goodness I am too mean to throw away old knife blades, as I have found these ideal for texturing wing and tail feathers.

PAINTING

After the texturing comes my favourite part, the painting. Once again reference is of the utmost importance, and I do not think you can have too much.

It is not unusual for me to have three or four books handy, referring to colour photographs for colour matching.

I use Winsor and Newton artists' watercolours which are fairly expensive, but last a fair time and are well known for their purity and quality of colour.

Again due to financial restraints I have used materials I already owned for my paintings, and most woodcarvers use acrylics, which once dried are waterproof. If my work were not all encased I would use acrylics myself.

All I can say about the painting is you must try to match the colouring as closely as possible, and keep some scraps of the wood you are using handy for testing colours.

Make sure you let the paint dry before deciding whether to mix a little bit of this and that with it, or just slap it on.

Painting is a very important part of my project and can ruin all the work already completed if hurried. Our favourite little robin redbreast could look as if he is standing behind a post-box. Their breasts are not red!

Be sure to keep all the colours you have mixed up until the very end, as there is always the chance you may need to touch up bits here and there. Unless you are experienced it can be difficult to re-match colours.

EYES

At this point we have a beautifully painted and carved bird minus beak, eyes and legs. I always leave the eyes until the bird is painted, as I find this tends to make positioning easier.

Once again I refer to my books and drawings, as any positional mistake here could leave me with a Marty Feldman look-alike, ruining all the previous work.

The only tip I can give here is to carefully cut out a paper eye of the right size with a sharp scalpel, colour it

Painting has been completed.

black, and keep positioning it until you are sure it is correct.

Once I'm happy with the position I make a pin prick in the centre of the eye which then gives me my centre point for drilling.

I do not have one of these nice slim lightweight drills so it's the good old-fashioned hand drill and my wife's hands to hold the bird in place while I perform this delicate operation.

The legs have been carved and fitted. The bird is ready for its box.

Ensure the hole is drilled smaller than you need. You can always take out more with your No 11 scalpel, but you cannot replace wood that has been removed.

Once the hole is drilled I make the eye. The only material I've ever used is Fimo modelling clay, which can be obtained at any good craft shop.

I roll a tiny piece of this into a ball and normally end up cutting bits off until I get the correct size. I then heat it in the oven to harden. Instructions are given on the packet for this.

When the cooking is done I let it cool off and then glue it in place. I have found the best paint to use on the eye is Humbrol black gloss as this gives a more natural glassy look.

To finish off you must not forget the little white highlight on the eye.

BEAK

The beak is made from any little offcut, according to my original drawings. I glue it onto the front of the bird's head with a little wood glue just to hold it in place while I draw around it.

As soon as I've done this I remove the beak, and using my No 11 scalpel I cut out the marked shape on the front of the bird to allow the beak to slot into the head.

This gives the bird a more realistic, authentic appearance. A bird's beak isn't just plonked onto the front of its head.

When the glue has set, I paint it with my Humbrol black gloss and when dry highlight with a little white paint across the top of the beak.

There are probably products on the market for making legs, but I cut thin strips of lime and sandpaper down to size and shape and cut to length when finished.

The claws I make from Fimo rolled out in very thin strips. Each claw is cut to length and then very carefully joined together with a sharp knife and moulded together.

If I need to shape the claws around a branch I do this by shaping around a suitable piece of metal rod and then pop it into the oven to cook.

The normal way of fixing is to drill into the body and glue into place, again referring to my drawings for correct positioning.

Allow plenty of drying time after gluing the legs as these are probably the most delicate and vulnerable parts of the project. Once fixed they can be painted, ensuring of course that the colour match is correct.

The birds are displayed in natural habitat, using plants and carved accessories, and put into boxes 200mm, 8in square with a glass front. Miniature lights, powered by batteries, enable them to be lit at night.

I am not an expert in this field by any means and have created a product of my very own by trial and error and a lot of patience.

I hope I have given you some idea of my way of working, and you can see that without spending lots of money on equipment you too can create a piece of wildlife art. ●

Winsor and Newton art supplies shop is at 51-2 Rathbone Place, London W1P 1AB. Tel: 0171 636 4231.

Terry Everitt is 42 and lives in Buxton, Norfolk. He worked in graphic design and spent his spare time producing detailed watercolour paintings of wildlife, particularly birds of prey. Self taught, he has exhibited his work at fairs throughout East Anglia. His driving ambition has been to produce an authentic, original piece of wildlife art with his *Naturebox*, to gain respect within the art world, and to be able to support a young family from his creation. Terry can be contacted for commissions at 110 Parmentergate Court, St John Street, Norwich, NR1 1PF Tel: 01603 465668

The finished collection
of reef pieces,
Denizens Of The Deep

DENIZENS OF

I began woodcarving in 1983 after being made redundant. I could not get another job, so I decided to take early retirement and do what I always wanted to do, carve. I joined weekend classes at the local college and was very fortunate with the teacher. She was Swiss and had served an apprenticeship back in her old country. She was also a fine artist, and under her tutelage I soon picked up the basics of woodcarving.

I started off carving free form and abstracts based on natural forms. After about five years of this I was given a pine (*Pinus spp.*) plank 15 x 2ft, 4.6 x 0.6m and told by the owner I could have it on condition I didn't cut it up. There was only one thing for it and that was a mural.

Living in Queensland I first thought I'd like to try the rainforest, but ended up carving the Barrier Reef. It took nine months to carve and after it was finished I was hooked on the reef.

The textures of the different corals were a challenge and it was obvious when I started the mural that most of the corals couldn't be reproduced with traditional tools. This was where my work experience took over. For nearly all my

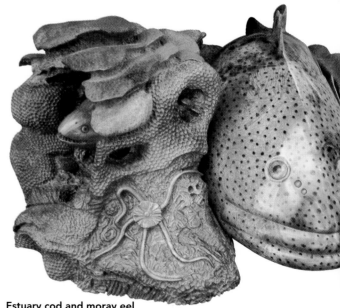

Estuary cod and moray eel

Arthur Clark
tells how
he recreated
the underwater
world of the Barrier
Reef off Australia

THE DEEP

working life I had been a toolmaker and the tool I continually used was a die sinker.

I bought a Dremel and went on to make and adapt rotary bits to suit the different textures found on the reef. After I finished the mural I decided to carve the Barrier Reef in three dimensions, and to call it *Denizens Of The Deep*.

Tropical timber

The timber I decided to use was the humble mango (*Mangifera indica*). Practically every backyard had one of these trees which had been planted by settlers when they first arrived in Queensland. After a number of years new breeds had been planted which developed superior fruit, so the old turpentine mango was being chopped down. This meant a plentiful and free supply of mango tree for me.

Some of the trees I was given were 5ft, 1.7m in diameter and I was able to create huge pieces for my project. I also discovered it was very colourful after oiling, and most importantly, it was very stable. If treated with oil while being carved, it didn't crack.

Reef creatures

The first piece I carved was an estuary cod. This was made from a whole tree and measured 6 x 4 x 2ft, 1.8 x 1.2 x 0.6m when completed. I decided from the start I would carve a fish or mammal as the dominant feature in each carving and leave wood around it to carve in the reef and smaller fish.

Then I carved a cow tailed ray. The log I used was 5ft, 1.5m in diameter so I was able to carve the ray life size. This piece, which was also surrounded by reef and smaller reef life, won first prize in the Queensland Working With Wood show in 1994. It measured 7ft, 2.1m long x 2ft, 0.6m high.

Next followed three bronze whaler sharks, 7ft, 2.1m long and made from two pieces of mango, and a full size green turtle. Two further pieces were a ray fish with cod and clam shell and reef, both of which were 6ft, 1.8m long x 3ft, 0.9m wide.

I carved a school of fish, which you can see in the background of the collection, from the roots of a large fig tree (*Ficus spp.*) which blew down in a storm and were ideal for this piece. I was fortunate in having the timber given to me as they were big buttress roots often found in the rainforest. The other reef pieces in the foreground were carved from offcuts of mango other people didn't want.

Creative process

In all my carvings of the reef, I always rough carve the dominant fish first. I am also careful not to undercut, and so I leave enough wood surrounding the fish to create coral and other creatures of the reef. I never undercut until I am sure the form I desire is correct. This way I can correct mistakes and alter the form if I want to.

I don't make a drawing or sketch prior to carving. I always mark the outlines of the dominant fish with a blue pen and carve down to those lines. The rest of the composition comes from the mind as the piece progresses.

So far this has worked out quite well. I've never been on the reef, mainly because I can't swim, so I depend on books, photos, videos and chats with people who have been on the reef to put me on the right track. Judging from public opinion, I think I have got it right.

I usually remove unwanted wood with an electric chainsaw, an Arbortech carving blade, and do the fine work with a Dremel, chisels and rifflers. My workshop consists of

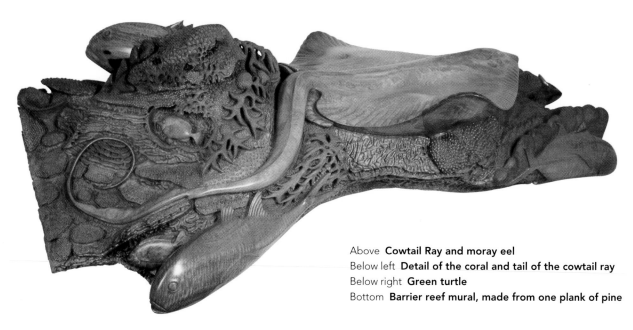

Above **Cowtail Ray and moray eel**
Below left **Detail of the coral and tail of the cowtail ray**
Below right **Green turtle**
Bottom **Barrier reef mural, made from one plank of pine**

carving I always paint what I've carved that day with a multi-purpose penetrating oil called Penetrol (obtainable in the UK but under a different brand name).

Despite the fact I carve green timber, the methods I use have kept the cracking to a minimum. If I do discover cracks, I fill them in with Timbermate, a filler which comes in numerous colours. I find I can match the colour of the timber with the right colour Timbermate filler and oil.

Denizens Of The Deep is now finished and it has taken me six years, carving an average of six hours a day. I've also painted a backdrop of the reef on a canvas measuring 25 x 5ft, 7.6 x 1.7m. I think I might carve smaller pieces in my next project. A collection of Australian birds would be great. ●

Above left **Cod fish and shovel nosed ray**
Below **Bronze whale sharks**

The textures of the different corals were a challenge

a 20 x 20ft, 6.1 x 6.1m shed and nothing else. The only tools I use are all hand-held.

I've turned a billiard room and a double garage on the side of the house into galleries so I can set *Denizens* out at home for people to view.

Carving stages

A tree usually arrives with a truck and crane. My first job is to chainsaw a flat bottom on the piece and remove the bark with the Arbortech carving blade, using the same tool to hollow out the bottom. This helps to relieve stress and prevent cracking.

I use a penetrating oil to seal the ends and bottom and leave it for about three months. By the end of the three months I've made up my mind about what it's going to be and I remove all the unwanted wood using the Arbortech.

When I get to the fine work I use chisels, rifflers, sanders and the Dremel rotary tools. At the end of each day's

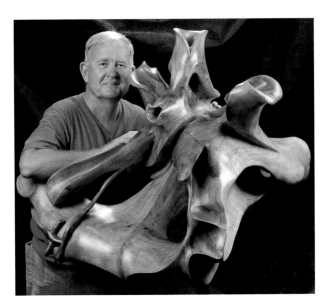

Arthur Clark emmigrated with his family to Australia from England in 1963. He has dabbled with woodturning and cabinet making since the age of 13 and started woodcarving lessons when he retired. He quickly drifted away from traditional styles and started experimenting with free form woodsculpture, taught with the aid of books. He is a member of Wood Artisans Guild of Queensland and continues to demonstrate and exhibit his work at Woodcraft shows throughout Australia.

SHELL OF AN IDEA

PROJECT

IN THE SECOND OF TWO ARTICLES ABOUT RECREATING THE AUSTRALIAN BARRIER REEF, ARTHUR CLARK EXPLAINS HOW HE CARVED A CLAM SHELL IN MANGO

This clam is just one of the many underwater creatures I carved during my work on *Denizens of the Deep*, a three dimensional representation of part of the Barrier Reef.

Below **The finished carving was buffed and oiled daily until the finish was satisfactory**
Centre **I used a chainsaw to create the flat bottom of the sculpture**

It is carved from a mango tree (*Mangifera indica*), many of which were planted by settlers when they first arrived in Queensland. The old turpentine mango is now being chopped down and replaced with superior fruit-growing species, which means there's plenty of free mango tree for me.

This mango tree had been deposited in my back yard and I removed all the bark using an Arbortech. The tree had been cut down for three months, so I didn't have to contend with the gooey substance usually associated with green trees while debarking, and the bark came off the tree quickly.

After de-barking, I stood the tree up so I could define where the top and bottom was going to be. The huge lump on the left hand side suggested a clam shell, so I decided that the

Removing bark from the mango tree

opposite side would be the bottom of the sculpture.

Next I used a chainsaw to create the flat bottom of the sculpture, and rolled it over to the workshop on pipe rollers. We had plenty of rain the day before, and the task wasn't easy, but with the help of friends and after a lot of grunting we managed to get it to the workshop. I decided to trim the log a bit with the chainsaw and the Arbortech.

While shaping the clam shell I was interrupted for a day by the TV crew of the Channel 10 Totally Wild Show, who had come to film *Denizens of the Deep*. Everything went well and the next day I was back to work on the clam shell, hollowing out the bottom of the sculpture with the Arbortech.

The first reason for this was to relieve the stress in the log and prevent

Below **Shaping the clam shell with the Arbortech**

cracking, and secondly to lighten the log for easier handling. After this, I used a multi-purpose finishing oil to seal the ends and bottom with two good coats. This helped to stabilise the log by letting it dry out slowly. I used this method on all the carvings in *Denizens of the Deep* and have had 100% success.

The next stage was to make a compartment, or tent, out of a plastic

Above **Hollowing out the bottom of the sculpture with the Arbortech**

car cover to contain the flying chips from the Arbortech, and there were plenty of them. All my neighbours have beautiful chip gardens courtesy of this project, and those neighbours who missed out requested I start a new one right away.

After I finished the general shape of the shell, I started marking the shell with carving lines using blue marker pen.

Up to this stage, I had used only the Arbortech and chainsaw. Next I began using Dremel rotary tools, chisels and riffler files to define more intricate details. It was then I decided what the composition surrounding the dominant feature of the clam shell would be.

Then I added reef, fish and shells to complement the clam. As I never draw the sculpture before carving, I left plenty of wood to work with, and designed the

whole piece just using the eye.

After carving each detail, I soaked it with multi-purpose wood oil to stop any cracking. It also gave a lovely matt finish. When I hold an exhibition, I go over all the sculptures with a damp cloth dipped in the same oil two hours before opening time.

When the carving was completed, I sanded where necessary, oiled daily and buffed with a lambswool buffing wheel until the finish was satisfactory.

The clam shell was the last of the

Above **After each detail was finished I soaked it with multi-purpose oil**
Below **Detail of the finished carving**

big pieces for *Denizens of the Deep*, which was shown at the Working With Wood Show at Sydney, NSW in July 1995. It took me from 1989 to 1995 to finish the entire Denizens project, working an average of six hours a day. ●

Arbortech supplied in the UK by
Bri Marc Associates, 8 Ladbroke Park,
Millers Road, Warwick CV34 5AE
Tel: 01926 493389

Dremel Multi tool is supplied in the UK
by Microflame Ltd, Vinces Road,
Diss, Norfolk IP22 3HQ
Tel: 01379 644 813

PROJECT · COD 'N' CHIPS

ARTHUR CLARK EXPLORES WAYS TO KEEP HIS GREEN WOOD FISH FROM DRYING OUT

I started carving after I retired eleven years ago. Since then I've tried various experiments to speed up the drying out period of timber between green and seasoned.

Not having the luxury of big sheds to dry timber the traditional way, I decided to study work done by old and native woodcarvers to find some answers to stress and cracking in green, round logs.

Take native canoes for example. The tree trunk is cut to the length required, de-barked, then the top of the log is cut flat and the hollowing out begins. The centre of the log is cut away to form the inner part of the canoe. This relieves stress and lessens the chance of cracks forming.

The early religious carvers followed an identical procedure by cutting a round log in half, hollowing out the flat side, and carving the half round front to form the figure required.

I took the information I had gleaned from earlier craftsmen and experimented with various modern oils. I was looking for an oil that would penetrate the timber and slow down the drying, to reduce the chances of cracking. The best oil I found is called Penetrol Multi Purpose Wood Oil and is manufactured here in Australia. I don't know if it is available elsewhere.

MANGO

The wood I used for this project was the humble mango fruit tree (*Mangifera indica*), which fortunately for me is plentiful in my home town of Bundaberg, Queensland.

I was able to obtain big trees, some 1.5m, 5ft in diameter which, as I wanted to carve the creatures of the reef full size, suited my requirements. Another bonus of mango wood is that

··

The mango log has been de-barked and part hollowed out with the Arbortech. The ends were squared with a chainsaw.

it is a very stable, medium density wood with a beautiful grain and colour.

I named the project *Denizens of the Deep* and I began carving in 1989. It is now one carving away from completion and when set out for showing, covers an area of 2.3 sq metres, 25 sq ft. There are more than 30 separate carvings covering coral reef, shells, and creatures found on the reef. (See previous articles, pages 74–79).

Four of the big fish carvings were worked from single trees, one measuring 2.1m, 7ft long and 1.37m, 4½ft wide, others measuring 1.8m, 6ft long and 1.2m, 4ft wide. Now on carvings this big, you would expect cracks to appear, but I have had only a few cracks which needed fillers.

I have tried two other timbers grown locally, but I'm firmly convinced that any medium density wood would work with this procedure.

To put my theory into practice, I decided to carve another fish and take photos to show how I carve green timber. I began with a mango log 1.5m, 5ft long x 610m, 24in diameter.

··

The ends of the log were sealed with oil to prevent cracking and the outline of the fish was drawn on. Waste wood was removed with the chainsaw and Arbortech.

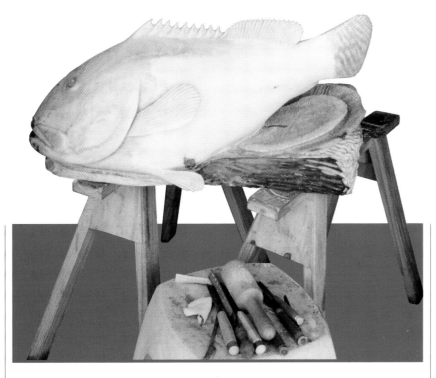

SAPWOOD

First I removed all of the sapwood using the Arbortech, squared the ends with a chainsaw, and oiled to seal.

I hollowed out the underside of the carving with the Arbortech. I endeavour always to take out as much of the centre of the log as possible. This relieves stress and helps to stabilise the log. When the hollowing out was finished, the log was soaked with oil, at least a couple of good coats to stop it cracking.

I next drew the outline of the fish onto the log and removed the excess wood with the Arbortech. The fish was oiled all over at the end of each day's carving.

As the fish and the reef came to life I started to carve the finer details using a chisel, riffler file and the Dremel. At this stage the worked and the previously oiled surface could clearly be

The fish and reef coming to life with fine detail added. The wood was oiled all over after each day's carving.

identified by the different colours of the wood. The colour of the carving got darker, and the oil eventually gave a beautiful patina.

BURNT SPOTS

With the carving completed I burned spots on the cod with a small gas torch, being careful not to play the torch on the wood for too long.

I recommend experimenting with this procedure, especially on different woods. I brought the torch in from a distance and let it play on the surface for a couple of seconds, which gave me the result I required.

I sanded the fish down to 300 grit, brushed on the oil and left it on for 15 minutes. I then wiped the surplus off

with an oil-dampened cloth. This was allowed to harden and dry overnight.

The next day I rubbed it back with a plastic scouring pad from the kitchen. This was repeated four times to build up the finish and the patina required.

I would strongly advise against using wire wool with some oils as the oil reacts with little bits of wire wool left in the wood, leaving rust marks.

The carving was now ready to be exhibited. The day before it went on show I rubbed it over with an oil dampened cloth and left it to dry overnight.

This whole project from the felling of the tree to the final polish took exactly six weeks. Three months later, there are no cracks or movement of any kind in the carving. ●

Arbortech supplied in the UK by BriMarc Associates,
8 Ladbroke Park, Millers Road,
Warwick CV34 5AE.
Tel: 01926 493389.

Dremel tools supplied in the UK by Microflame Ltd, Vinces Road,
Diss, Norfolk IP22 3HQ.
Tel: 01379 644813.

The completed cod darkened by the oil and gas torch.

WHAT A RAT

SARA WILKINSON SHOWS HOW SHE CARVED HER PET RAT BRUCE

Our pet rat, Bruce, lives in my workshop and as he has become a good friend, I decided to immortalise him by carving his portrait.

When carving an animal or a person it is essential to study the subject adequately, otherwise serious errors in anatomy can be made.

Obviously if you have an obliging and tame pet, life is made much easier, but otherwise it is important to look at good photographs or drawings, preferably taken from different angles.

It is extremely difficult to produce a life-like carving copying from just the front or side view.

This research is just as important when carving a stylised or abstract piece, otherwise the essence of the creature will not be captured.

Also, if the preparation is thorough and you have a firm picture in your mind of what you wish to achieve, the carving itself will emerge quickly and efficiently.

As my particular subject was lazy and docile I had ample opportunity for studying him. Bruce is hugely fat and 460mm, 18in from nose to the tip of his tail.

As I wished to stylise him rather than produce a replica I decided to elongate his head to make him more elegant than the original, and give him a wise and superior expression as he looked down his long nose.

I did not want him to look like a fluffy animal and therefore accentuated his muscles and the structure of his face.

I draped his tail around his head both as a decorative feature and because he sleeps squashed up with his long tail curled about him.

DRAWING

The first step was to draw the head out on paper. You do not have to be able to draw wonderfully, but it is important to have full sized working drawings to refer to. Much time is saved if you can trust your drawing enough to bandsaw exactly to your drawn outline.

Spend a little time selecting your timber carefully. I was going to use oak (*Quercus spp*) which would have produced a more robust carving but, not having any thick enough, settled for lime (*Tilia vulgaris*) of which I had plenty.

This gave me the advantage of being able to carve much more quickly, and as the piece was quite dark for lime, the colour was a pleasant mid brown.

Walnut (*Juglans spp*) would probably look attractive, and the colour life-like for a dark brown rat.

The timber measured 220 x 125mm, 8¾ x 5in and was 85mm, 3¼in thick. This allowed 40mm, 1⅝in extra in length for holding in the vice or attaching to a carving stand.

After transferring the design to the timber using carbon paper, the next step was to bandsaw the profile, cutting right up to the line. This process could easily be done with gouges instead, given the simplicity of the shape.

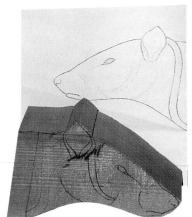

The drawn design transferred to the blank and bandsawn out.

Next I pencilled a centre line down the middle of the face. This is an essential step when carving anything symmetrical, especially a face, as it makes any unevenness of shape or features very apparent when the two sides are compared.

CARVING

The piece was now ready for carving. Using a gouge, I cut away the waste between the ears, leaving enough timber for the tail as it passed through them, and reduced the sides so the ears and tail were left standing high.

Next I rounded the corners, producing a virtual cone shape towards the nose.

The muscles and definite lines and structure of the face were then carved in. I left the top very flat and accentuated the cheeks and nose. At this stage you must leave large enough bumps for the eyes, including enough for the eyelids.

The original drawing.

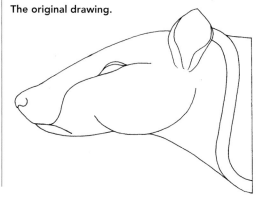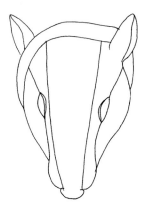

Above **The area between the ears has been removed and the sides reduced.**
Below **When defining the head shape enough wood must be left for the eyes and eyelids.**
Bottom **The eyes carved without irises or pupils.**
Bottom right **The mouth is underneath the face.**

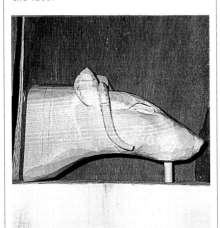

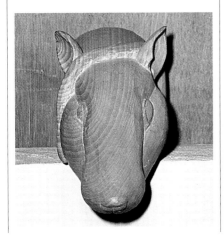

Next I carved the features. The ears were positioned so they faced neither to the front nor side but half way between. Imagine them positioned where the corners would have been.

In shaping ears, it is helpful to think of them as delicate, hollowed shells, but do not over thin them as the structure is weak due to short grain.

I carved the eyes with lids but did not indicate the iris or pupil as I wished to keep the lines simple.

Eyes always present a problem to the carver as the eyeball is smooth, yet some people think the expression looks blank if the iris and pupil are not defined. One solution to this is to carve an indentation to represent the pupil, but this must remain a matter of personal choice.

I carved the nose and mouth taking care not to make them look like a stuffed toy. The mouth is almost underneath the face, and I turned the corners down to avoid him looking too cute.

TAIL

Finally I rounded the tail over, and although I had intended adding some cross hatching texture, like the original,

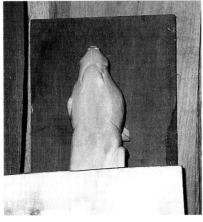

The finished trophy-style portrait.

the grain itself added enough detail.

As the carving was to be finished from the tool and not sanded, I then checked it over for dull patches and to make sure the detail was crisp.

Sharp tools are needed for this, before cutting off the excess timber with a fine-toothed saw.

Two coats of Danish oil and some beeswax polish finished Bruce's portrait.

I designed him to be mounted on the wall like a trophy, but he looks quite good upended looking up at the stars. ●

Sara Wilkinson was born in Surrey in 1954 and was brought up in Cornwall and Devon.
She trained in London as a nurse, then did an English degree. She later studied furniture making and carving at The London College of Furniture (Guildhall University) and taught at Paddington College.
She has undertaken furniture commissions, but now concentrates on carving when time allows, especially sculptures of people.
Sara lives in Wivenhoe, Essex, and teaches carving and woodwork part-time at Braintree College, adult education evening classes and a social services centre.

My husband laughed and said "How long will this one last then?" His question was based on the numerous hobbies I'd taken up and dropped again in the past – pottery, rowing, painting, aerobics, sketching, swimming. "No", I said, "This one's different. This time I'm going to stick at it. I promise I won't get bored." I was referring to my new-found hobby, woodcarving.

For some unknown reason, I had picked up a magazine from the newsstand, and quickly flicked through it. There was a report of a show where the competitors had to carve a big cat. I could do that, I thought. Now how do I start?

A month or so later, the same magazine revealed the theme for the 1992 show. Called *Denizens of the Deep*, entrants could carve any marine creature. I decided to do it and just had to convince my husband to buy me a set of gouges as an early Christmas present. Eventually he agreed, and within weeks we were driving down to Perth to collect an elm (*Ulmus spp*) burr.

I decided to carve an octopus and, after buying a book on identifying wood, elm burr seemed the most obvious choice to represent the skin pattern. I collected as many photographs of octopuses as possible, and began.

By this time, my family and friends all thought I was completely mad. I chiselled frantically at a lump of gnarled, slightly rotten wood telling them all it was going to be an octopus.

A few months later, I had proved my critics wrong and indeed had carved an octopus. Even the dog was impressed. It was completed just in time for the show and I was very proud to win a runner-up prize.

Learning from scratch

I have been a graphic artist since leaving school 11 years ago. So I am used to working in two dimensions. I had dabbled with pottery and modelling in clay, but lacked experience in working with a medium which did not allow for many mistakes.

With this in mind, I decided to make a clay model first. This helped me get to know the subject well and work out what certain areas looked like in three dimensions. I used photos and the occasional sketch as reference.

Learning to sharpen the tools along the way, and working with a very unforgiving wood, meant the finished piece took longer than it might take me now. Elm burr has a tendency to be brittle, and that lovely crisp, tooled finish seen on so many carvings evaded me. So I settled for hour upon hour of sanding to leave my octopus as smooth as a baby's bottom.

I chose holly (*Ilex spp*) for the eyes, as I wanted them to contrast with the burr and to catch the viewer's attention. They were carved into a cylinder and attached to an electric drill. Then, like a very simple lathe, I turned the dowels using sandpaper to grind the surface, until the desired shape was achieved. The pupil was filled with black wax filler.

Finally, it was finished off with several coats of linseed oil and wax polish. I kept the wood well-oiled throughout the carving, to prevent small shakes appearing around the numerous knots. I filled any which did appear with mahogany (*Swietenia macrophylla*) wood stopping. With hindsight, I should have chosen a black filler, as this tones in much better with the burr.

Super Puma

My projects are usually inspired by wildlife, whether they are paintings, sketches or three-dimensional work. So my next request was a little bit unusual. I was asked to carve a Super Puma for a company in Aberdeen. Not a big cat, but a helicopter.

Although I was a bit unsure of the commission I accepted and, at the client's request, bought a piece of English walnut (*Juglans regia*). In the end the commission turned out to be a relatively easy project. Excellent reference material was available and I did not have to worry about

bringing the carving alive. Essentially, it was an exercise in techniques and I learned a lot from it.

The main rotor blades had to be free to turn. I accomplished this quite easily by using a brass pin inserted into the body of the helicopter, and a brass sheath glued inside a hole in the centre of the rotor blades. A liberal coating of grease gave a smooth movement.

The whole assembly was kept in place by a carved cap glued on top of the brass pin. I made the logo from brass shimming paper, carefully cut with a scalpel and glued in place.

I wanted to show the helicopter in flight with the landing gear down. So I selected a granite base to represent the North Sea on a rough day, with the suggestion that the helicopter was performing a search operation. It was finished with Danish oil, dulled down with steel wool and several coats of wax. My client was very pleased with the result.

First Prize

My third and most recent carving, entitled *Little Big Ears*, won its class and was the Editor's Choice at the 1994 National Woodworker Show.

It depicts an African elephant mother and calf. The calf wriggles and jumps about, full of the joys of youth, while the mother, wise in her mature years, watches over her

WILD ●SPIRIT

FEATURE

Inspired by wildlife, Lesley McKenzie aims to capture the spirit of the subject in her work

Left ***Little Big Ears*** won a silver and a gold medal at the National Woodworker Show, taking Editor's Choice and third Best Finish prizes
Below **The common octopus won a bronze medal at the National Woodworker Show. It was my first carving and took around 150 hours to complete**

offspring, lending a gentle trunk when required.

I chose elm burr for its beauty when polished. Any difficulties experienced in carving this wood were well worth the end result. The carving was not going to be highly detailed, so I could have used any wood with good figuring.

I wanted to portray the intelligence and gentleness of the elephants, while giving the impression of strength and life. I used photos for reference, selecting a leg here and an ear there until I was happy with the overall composition. I made a couple of rough sketches and kept all the photos to hand, constantly referring to them as the carving progressed.

Handy work

I had not yet acquired expensive power tools and bandsaws, so I could not cut to a profile, as suggested by many carvers. The burr I used was quite literally 'in the round', so I started at the top and worked down. No measuring was required, I gauged the whole carving by eye.

Other beginners need not despair. A lack of power tools is not necessarily a disadvantage and can be just the opposite. The blocky, square carvings often produced by some beginners and professionals alike are, to my mind, a direct result of bandsawing.

The carver feels apprehensive about removing too much wood for fear of spoiling the carving. The freedom to explore your way into the wood is taken away and the result is restrained and often appears lifeless.

Throw away the bandsaw and the carver is forced to think about their subject. You notice, taking the elephants as an example, how the left side reacts to the right side relaxing, what the bone structure looks like under the skin, the weight of the muscles when resting, compared to their strength when tense.

Slowly, a whole new dimension arises and carving is more enjoyable. It becomes part of you. You have created it. Having said this, if I had the appropriate power tools, I would use them. I do not doubt their value in removing waste wood quickly and relatively effortlessly.

I don't think you need to be able to draw to carve, but you do need to be able to imagine a three-dimensional shape. It is good to close your eyes and think of your subject as it would appear to a blind person. You soon realise how much more studying you have to do to fill in the blanks.

Rotten disguise

Coming down off my soap box, I did experience a few problems.
The burr I had chosen had been lying outside for a long time, so bits of it were soft and rotten. Unfortunately, you don't always find this out until you are merrily carving away. As a result, the composition was

changed slightly and, I'm pleased to say, for the better.

I decided not to disguise the rotten areas, as they were part of the wood's character and charm. I filled only small shakes, this time with black wood stopping.

There were, however, two areas of rot that had to be patched. These were quite large, and meant part of the mother's front and hind legs were missing, distracting from the overall form. I patched them with a small piece of burr carved to shape, and glued in place.

I carved the tusks from holly and glued them into holes made in the burr. I then gave the tusks a used look by giving them a light stain of linseed oil.

I finished the carving off with a coat of shellac sanding sealer, to stop the subsequent coats of wax polish from sinking into the wood. This gave the elephants a wonderful deep lustre without being overly glossy. The success of this finishing method was confirmed by winning the Henry Flack Third Best Finish award at the National Woodworker Show.

Over the past year, I have been showing my work at the Scottish Native Timbers Exhibition. It is organised by Ian Brodie of the Bio-Forest Consultancy and its aim is to promote the use of Scottish sustainable timbers in craft and industry.

They invited me to do a four-day carving demonstration at the Royal Highland Show in Edinburgh and although I can hardly class myself as an expert, I can give some instruction on the basics of getting started.

After two years I have proved my interest in this hobby is still strong. I hope to dedicate more time to it this year. I now have a small workshop set up in my garden shed where I used to breed rabbits (but that's another story) and I have a few more gouges to add to my collection.

My husband now accepts carving as a serious hobby. But I wonder if he would have agreed to it if he'd known about the trips round the country for shows and competitions. Now where did I put that address in America? ●

Lesley McKenzie was born in 1967 and has lived just outside Aberdeen all her life. Self-taught, and inspired by wildlife, she started carving two years ago in response to a competition where she won a runner up prize. Her most recent success was at the 1994 National Woodworker Show, where she won a bronze and silver medal and a gold for Editor's Choice. Supported by her husband, she hopes to make carving her full-time occupation in the future.

The *Super Puma* helicopter, was comissioned by a company in Aberdeen. It took around 80 hours to complete

MODERN MADONNA

JOHN DWYER DESCRIBES HOW HE CARVED A PROCESSIONAL MARY AND CHILD FOR WESTMINSTER ABBEY

In the summer of 1994 a colleague of mine invited me to view the restoration work in progress at Westminster Abbey. The Abbey has been used for the burial and coronation of the kings and queens of England for over 900 years and took more than 500 years to complete. I was therefore delighted to have a closer look at the building.

Below **The Abbey's west front built 1734–45 by Nicholas Hawksmoor.**
Bottom **One of the 90 figures in the Henry VII chapel. The woman is pregnant and probably represents Mary or Elizabeth.**

After climbing the scaffold within the Henry VII chapel I was staggered to find such a quality and quantity of fine stone carving. I remember leaving the Abbey somewhat overwhelmed by the craftsmanship of centuries past.

I returned on several other occasions and on one such visit decided to pop into St Margaret's. This church is part of the Abbey and is a 'Royal Peculiar' which means it is not under the direct authority of the Archbishop of Canterbury but of the Queen.

I thought it odd that this church should have been built so close to the Abbey, but the Sacristan enlightened me by explaining it was built in the later half of the 11th century for the lay folk of Westminster – the Benedictine monks of the Abbey not wanting to be disturbed while singing Divine Office.

It was at this time I learned he was looking for someone to carve a processional image for the Society of Our Lady of Pew.

Above **The finished processional image of Our Lady of Pew.**
Left **The Lady of Westminster Cathedral.**

Of course I jumped at the opportunity of carving something that would be used in the Abbey so I passed on samples of my work and drawings and was accepted. The image was to be completed by the summer of '95, ready for a June service where it would be welcomed into the Abbey.

THE LADY OF PEW

It wasn't until late September that I received more details of the image to be carved, which was frustrating because I was eager to start.

It was to be of Our Lady of Pew, an ancient title for The Virgin Mary, and loosely based on the painted alabaster statue of the Lady of Westminster Cathedral.

The word Pew is thought to derive from a French word for power, the title going back to the 11th century. The new mother however, was to be more feminine and elegant than the stocky alabaster figure, and the child less spindly. It was also to be of the approximate same size as the alabaster statue (900mm, 3ft high).

The alabaster figure is really a deep relief to be set against a wall or pillar, and both the arms and legs of the mother are foreshortened. The processional image was to be seen and carved in the round.

REDESIGNING

I photographed and measured the alabaster figure which, according to the cathedral, was carved in the early 15th century by the Nottingham School of Alabaster. In this carving the mother looks directly at the viewer and the child at the mother, but I felt the composition would be more interesting if they looked at one another.

After all, I thought, emphasising their relationship would make it easier for people to identify with them since relationships are such an essential part of living.

I made some half-size drawings using several books, but found E. J. Tangerman's *Complete Guide to Woodcarving* especially helpful in ensuring my human proportions were correct.

The faces of my figures have smaller than average mouths (fractionally greater than one eye length) and slightly larger eyes and noses.

These are proportions that give the face an expression of powerful quietness and calm, and were used by the Greeks, Renaissance artists and even Pablo Picasso (with variations).

I passed my drawings on to the committee of the society and waited until December for their approval.

MAQUETTES

Before attempting the full size image I first made a clay, and then wooden, maquette. I find doing so helps me grasp the form and dimensions of the work in hand and also irons out any problems, known or unknown.

I worked on the maquette in the evenings and at weekends and after completion presented it to the committee for their comments and suggestions.

Top **The clay maquette with wooden armature and wire.**

Above **The completed wooden maquette.**

THE FINAL CUT

By March all the finer details were clarified. I made full-size drawings and ordered the wood from the suppliers. After the finer details had been confirmed I was confident of what I was to carve and approached the work with renewed vigour and enthusiasm.

The wood I chose was lime (*Tilia vulgaris*) for its workability, light colour and reasonable weight. Weight was an important factor in the design process, this being a processional image, carried on a bearer.

I felt the best way of overcoming the weight problem was to opt for a hollow construction. This entailed laminating four sections of lime together which allowed me to remove a great deal of timber from the centre of the figures before carving began.

Using laminates also allowed the growth rings to be alternated, thereby improving the stability of the timber, and meant I could use kiln-dried timber. The dryness of kiln-dried timber is not guaranteed when over 100mm, 4in thick.

The four sections of lime, 1000 x 475 x 100mm, 40 x 18 x 4in, duly arrived and I was quietly stunned at their 102kg, 16st weight. The full-size drawings were transferred onto the timbers using carbon paper and the waste cut away using a bandsaw.

What was left weighed 10st, 64kg and I seriously wondered if the image would ever approach a comfortable weight for carrying.

POWERGOUGE

I did not glue the laminates together but temporarily fixed them in position with 40 x 10mm, 1⅝ x ⅜in dowels, and began roughing out the basic forms with a Powergouge, a 115mm, 4½in tungsten-tipped disk used in a small angle grinder.

The temporary dowelling allowed access to remove more waste from the insides at a later stage since I had left a

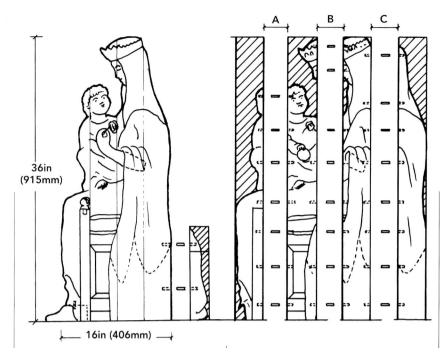

36in
(915mm)

|← 16in (406mm) →|

A   B   C

Above **Arm joint, additional robe sections, turned ball for chair and jointing of feet.**
Below **Full size drawings transferred to timber.**
Bottom **Bandsawn sections of lime open at joint A. Dowels and marking out of chair.**

Method of construction and dowels used to hold the laminates together.

Right **The child in the making, mother's face not yet started.**
Far right **The child glued together but looking like a gremlin at this stage.**

good deal of timber as a margin for error. There were many deep hollows and curves to be carved and the last thing I wanted to do was break into the cavity.

ROUTER

The weight of the timber was such that it remained stable without clamps, but I screwed a length of 50 x 50mm, 2 x 2in timber to the underside of the sections and held them in a Black & Decker Workmate just to be safe.

After the initial roughing out I separated the sections at joint B and focused on the child. I began to develop his form with a portable router (Bosch POF 500) fitted with tungsten burrs. I then did the same for the mother. Use only purpose-made burrs for this task and wear goggles and a mask.

HOLLOWING

I then opened each of the figures up at joints A and C and removed more timber from their centres, heads included, making both of them hollow with a 50mm, 2in, skin.

This had the great advantage, other than that of lessening the weight, of alleviating tensions in the wood that might have caused shakes and splits to appear at a later stage.

Each of the figures was glued and clamped together but remained free at joint B. This allowed me to pull them apart whenever I needed better access to the child's face, ears and neck, something I had learned would be useful from the maquette.

As you can see from the pictures, I needed every clamp available to glue the figures effectively and could really have done with strap cramps, the kind used on lorries for holding cargo in place.

CARVING THE FACES

Putting my mechanical aids to one side I picked up my chisels and began working on the faces and the child's hands and feet.

Faces are an extremely important part of any figure. After all, we have all studied them, consciously or unconsciously all our lives, so we are all

Mother and child being glued and clamped.

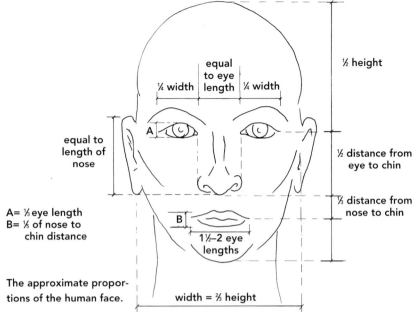

equal to eye length

¼ width | equal to eye length | ¼ width

½ height

equal to length of nose

A

½ distance from eye to chin

⅓ distance from nose to chin

A= ⅓ eye length
B= ⅓ of nose to chin distance

B

1½–2 eye lengths

The approximate proportions of the human face.

width = ⅔ height

experts on how a face should look.

If a face is carved badly it ruins the overall effect of the figure. Also, the face plays the major part in determining the mood of a figure and therefore should be thought about and carved with great care and much patience.

I found learning the basic proportions of the human face absolutely invaluable before carving them. These proportions are only approximate but serve as a foundation to carving faces well and are a constant reference for work in progress.

However, even with these proportions at hand, the face develops slowly, especially if you have a particular mood in mind for it to impart.

After defining the lips, nose and eyes with chisels I found the easiest way of getting the subtler forms of the face was to use rifflers, especially the hooked riffler.

In general a man's face is slightly broader than that of a woman's, while the woman has thicker and longer lips and larger eyes.

But remember if it looks right, it is right. It may not be perfect anatomically speaking but if it expresses what you want it to, in a convincing manner, 99% of the work is complete.

ROBES

I then resigned myself to working on the robes. I had encountered some difficulty with the maquette in trying to make the robes look realistic and this was a concern to me.

However, I eventually found I was

able to carve a more convincing cloth if I focused on the shadows they cast and not on the material itself.

I don't know why this approach helped me but it did. It may be that I had been relying too heavily on my sketches for the maquette instead of simply going with the flow.

Where the cloth was to gather and fold at the foot of the chair I glued and dowelled more sections of lime about 300mm, 12in high and 75mm, 3in deep. These were then carved and blended into the rest of the robe.

After the robes had been completed I removed further waste from the centre of the carving with the Powergouge. This brought the timber skin to a uniform 50–75mm, 2–3in thickness.

I then sealed the centre with a couple of coats of sanding sealer and glued the mother and child together.

CHAIR, CROWN AND BALL

The chair is of simple design incorporating raised panels and two turned balls, glued and dowelled in position. I did not want the chair to be too fussy as this could have detracted from the softer and quieter tones of the figures.

The pattern of the crown is based upon oak leaves signifying personal distinction and, like the flower, was gilded with gold leaf.

Unlike the cathedral Madonna who holds a lily in her hand, the Abbey Madonna holds a rose. The lily signifies purity whereas the rose specifically associates the Madonna with England.

The ball the child is blessing represents the world.

HANDS, FEET AND FLOWER

I carved the mother's hands from separate pieces of timber to avoid short grain which would have made the fingers extremely fragile. For the same reason I did likewise with the flower and Madonna's feet.

The hands were glued and dowelled securely into two large sockets formed by the overhanging robes. I made the sockets smaller than the thickness of the forearms and then increased their size until a snug fit was achieved.

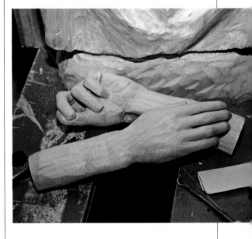

The mother's hands.

The easiest way I found of doing this was by rubbing pencil lead over the forearms and pushing them into the sockets. This left a mark on all the tight spots in the sockets which I duly removed with a gouge.

I slid the flower through a 7mm, ¼in diameter hole bored between the forefinger and thumb still touching each other, which is not correct, but it

The mother's face softened by rifflers and abrasive cloth.

added strength to a vulnerable place, bearing in mind the figures will be constantly moved from place to place and touched by the public.

The feet were then glued and dowelled into position using the same technique as with the forearms.

Now complete, the carving weighed 38kg, 6st which can be comfortably carried by two or more people.

RUBBING DOWN

Next came the many, many, mind-numbing hours of rubbing down using Hermes Rb 406 J-Flex, an abrasive cloth I find comfortable to use and long lasting. I used four grades starting with the most coarse 80, then the 120, 240 and finally 320 grit.

The carving was then rubbed over with a damp cloth to raise the grain, allowed to dry and then rubbed down again with the 320 grit.

On request my name, date, and the words "*Ut umum sint*" were carved on the back of the mother's robe. Ut umum sint is Latin for "that all may be one", church unity being the main concern of the society.

Not including the bleaching or gilding the Madonna and child took approximately 240 hours to construct and carve.

BLEACHING

The committee were extremely cautious when I requested the image be bleached white but decided the artist knew best and gave their consent.

I explained it would emphasise the purity and divinity of the subject as well as be in harmony with the white Portland limestone of the Abbey itself. Also, I found the natural figure of the wood detracted from the softer forms of the carving.

Such bleaching is obviously a contentious issue and different people will have different views, but it should be remembered that carvings have been painted for thousands of years.

I used Rustin's two-part bleach to whiten the figures. It was easy to use, part A was applied first and left for approximately 20 minutes and then part B was applied and left overnight.

The bleaching process was then stopped with an application of white vinegar diluted in water. I had tested the bleach earlier and therefore knew how long to leave it to achieve the desired effect.

Once the bleach was neutralised I rubbed the figures down again with the 320 grade abrasive. Then I applied several coats of white polish and finally buffed the carving up with white wax.

As far as I am aware this is the only white processional image carved in wood in existence, but would like to hear from any reader who knows of another.

JUNE SERVICE

At the summer service the statue was seen by the public and the society's members for the first time. People immediately warmed to the Madonna and child and thought them beautiful and serene.

In the service the processional image was blessed, the first time this has happened in the Abbey since 1536.

The Lady of Pew processional image is kept in the Lady Chapel (Henry VIII), and can be seen at the society services in the Abbey which take place throughout the year.

I have been asked on many occasions if I was pleased with the end result. The answer is yes but, as is always the case, it could be better. ●

Complete Guide to Woodcarving by E.J. Tangerman is published by Sterling Publishing Co. Inc., New York, USA. Available in the UK from GMC Publications, 166 High Street, Lewes, E. Sussex BN7 1XU. Tel: 01273 488005. Price £11.99 plus p&p £2.50 (UK) £3.50 (overseas).

Powergouge available from Bowman (UK) Ltd, Peel House, 98 Old Heath Road, Colchester, Essex CO1 2HB. Tel: 01206 792268.

Black & Decker Ltd, 210 Bath Road, Slough, Berkshire SL1 3YD. Tel: 01753 511234.

Robert Bosch Ltd, PO Box 98, Broadwater Park, North Orbital Road, Denham, Uxbridge, Middlesex UB9 5HJ. Tel: 01895 834466.

Hermes abrasives available from CSM Trade Supplies, 95–6 Lewes Road, Brighton, E. Sussex BN2 3QA. Tel: 01273 600434.

Rustin's Ltd, Waterloo Road, London NW2 7TX. Tel: 0181 450 4666.

John Dwyer is a London-based sculptor. For commissioned work please contact 0171 635 6815, or write to 23 Astbury Road, Peckham, London SE15 2NL

FEATURE ●NATURAL

Vic Wood talks to Australian sculptor Silvio Apponyi

M onumental mason and journeyman sculptor Silvio Apponyi does not require an elaborate introduction. He is well known in Australia and has had work exhibited in Britain, Germany and the USA. Silvio was born in 1949 in Germany and emigrated to Australia as a small child. He studied at the South Australian School of Art, before going on to study art on a scholarship programme offered by the West German Government.

Once you are acquainted with his working style and process, you realise how all the chips of stone and wood take shape under his careful touch, and are transformed into lively works.

To survive as a carver, Silvio worked as a letter cutter, carving inscriptions on tombstones as a monumental mason. He does not regret this work, neither is he ashamed of it, as it broadened his outlook and opened up new horizons.

Silvio prefers to work in wood, maybe because of his childhood experience of making wooden boats, and other objects. "I like to work with wood because each piece has its own character," he told me. There is an element of chance

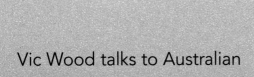

Main picture **Wedge Tail Eagle with Chick** in jarrah (*Eucalyptus marginata*)
Left **Squid and Prey** in red cedar and marble
Right **Ringtail Possum** in red cedar and bronze

PASSION

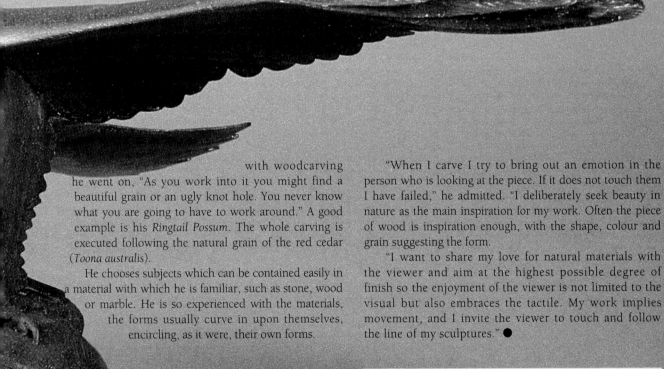

'I try to bring out an emotion in the person who is looking at the piece'

with woodcarving he went on, "As you work into it you might find a beautiful grain or an ugly knot hole. You never know what you are going to have to work around." A good example is his *Ringtail Possum*. The whole carving is executed following the natural grain of the red cedar (*Toona australis*).

He chooses subjects which can be contained easily in a material with which he is familiar, such as stone, wood or marble. He is so experienced with the materials, the forms usually curve in upon themselves, encircling, as it were, their own forms.

"When I carve I try to bring out an emotion in the person who is looking at the piece. If it does not touch them I have failed," he admitted. "I deliberately seek beauty in nature as the main inspiration for my work. Often the piece of wood is inspiration enough, with the shape, colour and grain suggesting the form.

"I want to share my love for natural materials with the viewer and aim at the highest possible degree of finish so the enjoyment of the viewer is not limited to the visual but also embraces the tactile. My work implies movement, and I invite the viewer to touch and follow the line of my sculptures." ●

'I want to share my love
for natural materials
with the viewer'

Top *Green Tree Frog* in English boxwood
Above *Spiney Tailed Gecko* in English boxwood (*Buxus sempervirens*) with an acacia (*Umbellularia californica*) inlay
Above right *Pignose Tortoise*, an endangered species in red gum (*Eucalyptus camaldulensis*)
Right *Frog with Centipede* in English boxwood

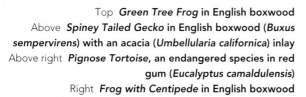

Silvio Apponyi can be contacted for commissions at
7 Bellevue Drive, Bellevue Heights, South Australia 5050.
Phone/Fax +61 8 277 1812

OVEN READY BIRD

A GARDEN TREE AND A DOMESTIC MICROWAVE OVEN HELPED DAVID MACKENZIE CREATE A CARVING OF A WILD BIRD

The Dartford Warbler is a small bird that is becoming increasingly rare in the British Isles. Its claim to fame is that it is the only warbler which lives in Britain all year round. All other warblers show a great deal more sense and go south to warmer countries for the winter. It is found mainly in the south in open heath lands and gorse covered hills.

MATERIALS

The laburnum (*Laburnum anagyroides*) is a small flowering tree that originated in the mountains of Europe. It is grown in parks and gardens for the abundance of bright yellow hanging flowers it bears in the spring. It is an enduring hardwood with light, creamy coloured sapwood, and dark, coarse-grained heartwood.

It is sometimes found in antique furniture where cross sections called oysters are inlaid into a surface as a decorative feature, and it is also used for turning small decorative objects.

I got the log from a friend who cut down a tree in his garden. This is a good source of logs for carving, the only problem being they require seasoning. The good news is they are usually free, so it is possible to experiment without fear of ruining an expensive piece of wood.

Another good reason for obtaining logs rather than sawn chunks, is that natural logs still have bark, and more importantly sapwood. The sapwood in some species is a different colour and this can be used to advantage in carvings.

Yew (*Taxus baccata*) and laburnum are good examples of wood with this colour variation, and this was one of the reasons I chose to carve this subject in laburnum.

Using native woods from a known source removes any fears about the ecological results of our hobby, and seasoning need not be a problem as it is possible to dry it out in a reasonable time in a microwave oven.

....

The completed Dartford warbler.

Bark and sapwood are visible here. The grain allows the beak and tail to retain their strength while pointing at different angles.

OVEN READY

There are several methods of drying or seasoning logs. They can be air dried, which is the traditional method and takes approximately one year for each 25mm, 1in thickness, or they can be kiln dried, which is usually beyond the resources of most DIY enthusiasts.

Another way is to use PEG (polyethylene glycol) which takes approximately 1 week for every 6mm, ¼in thickness plus another week to drain.

The fourth way and the method I used for this carving, was to dry it in a microwave oven, which takes approximately one day, depending on the moisture content of the log.

Newly harvested logs contain a high percentage of water, and the process of removing the moisture from the cells of the wood is known as seasoning.

If logs are allowed to dry naturally, and the end grain is not sealed, the wood will split at the ends. This is because the ends dry quicker than the middle, the wood shrinks and the log splits. In a microwave, the log dries from the inside, so the wood does not split, although it might distort a little.

When using a microwave, the heating does not penetrate much more than 38mm, 1½in into the wood, so it is best left until after the carving has been bandsawn.

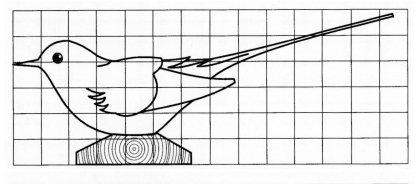

Similarly, do not wait until too much detailed carving has been done, but dry it as soon as the initial shapes have been sawn out from the log.

It is a matter of common sense to put as small a piece into the oven as you can manage, while making sure you haven't invested too much work already. I have yet to lose a piece, but better safe than sorry.

The drying times quoted below are for a small microwave. If a larger microwave is used these times might be too long. It is best to try it on a piece of scrap wood first.

After the shape has been sawn, make a note of the weight and put it in the microwave for 30 seconds only. After it is taken out, let it cool for half an hour. The cooling period is important because it is possible to make the middle of the log smoulder if too much heat is applied at one time.

For safety reasons the drying is done in only short bursts and allowed to cool completely between each heating session. If too much heat is applied a sizzling sound will come from the log and steam will escape from the ends.

After the first heating and cooling cycle the log should be weighed again and the weight compared with the first reading. Some of the moisture will have been driven off and it will be lighter.

Repeat this process until the wood stops losing weight by any noticeable amount. For this carving this did not happen until after five heating cycles.

Next, double the heating time to one minute and check for any weight loss. It is possible the moisture content will again fall and the scales will register a drop in weight.

The warbler carving required a series of four one minute cycles until the log was completely dry. The weight at the start was 362g and after the heating process it weighed 310g.

DESIGN

This description is a generic method for making any small carving. It is not necessary to use my drawings, and if you want to create a carving to your own design you can use the method described.

To begin with decide which bird to carve. When the subject has been chosen the next step is to make several sketches from books or observation, showing the side and top views.

Make a model of the selected subject from modelling clay. It is not strictly necessary to do this, but I find it helps solve some of the problems posed when working in three dimensions.

The Dartford warbler is 125mm, 5in from beak to tail, so the model was made life size. It is always difficult to decide on the pose, and a number of problems must be considered.

If the subject has a long straight tail and a thin beak it is imperative neither of these thin sections is across the grain, as this would mean they would break easily. This was difficult in this case because beak and tail were at different angles. To remedy this, I chose a piece of wood from a Y-shaped log which had two different directions for the grain.

Another problem was that as with most small birds, the Dartford warbler has very thin legs which would not support the weight of the body if they were made of wood. This meant the bird had to be positioned so some of the body weight was supported by whatever it was perched on.

Although it was possible to use a position where the bird was at rest, so the legs were completely hidden under

Above **Plan and top view of a pied wagtail.**

the body, the option I chose put the legs in full view, but most of the body weight was supported on the perch, and one of the legs was left free of the base.

I made a Plasticine model so the general shape and proportions of the bird could be studied, avoiding excessive detail which was not appropriate to its function as a guide.

When the model looked satisfactory, I used it to remake the drawings onto a 25mm, 1in sq grid, both from the side view and from the top. These were used as a guide to sawing out the wooden carving.

I cut a 75mm, 3in thick slice from the laburnum log with a bandsaw. The grain changed direction, which was an important feature in this carving.

From the squared up drawing I made a cardboard template of the side view by tracing, and this was used to transfer the shape onto the side of the log.

Plasticine model.

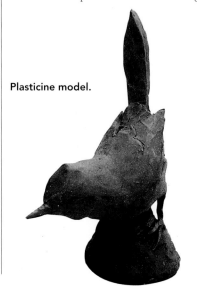

Above **The bird was drawn onto the Y section log so the tail and beak were both along the grain.**
Below **Roughed out carving ready for the oven.**

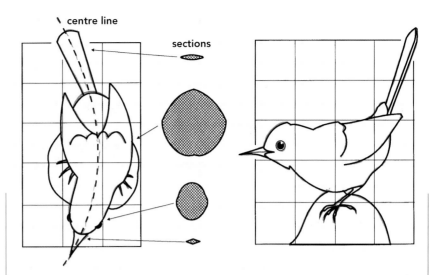

centre line

sections

centre line

Above **More drawings are made from the clay model.**
Below **A centre line is drawn on the bandsawn blank.**

centre line

The template was positioned so the top of the head was in the light, creamy coloured sapwood layer around the edge of the log. The idea of this was the body of the bird would be principally made from the dark coloured heartwood, but the top of the head was a contrasting colour.

I drew around the template, and made the initial cuts, following loosely around the pencil lines with a bandsaw, making an allowance of about 1.5mm, ¹⁄₁₆in, for errors. The view from the top was then drawn onto this shape and cut around with a coping saw.

At this stage the green wood was zapped in the microwave to dry it out. When this was successfully done, I drew a centre pencil line around the profile which was used when carving to ensure the shape was kept symmetrical. This was a useful guideline which was redrawn as it was cut away during carving.

THE CARVING

The bandsawing left a rather chunky looking shape with lots of corners on

it, so the next task was to round all the sharp edges where appropriate. To do this, I used a mixture of rasps and chisels, but I found the most useful tool for roughing out quickly was a rotary rasp on a flexible drive connected to a power drill.

As work proceeded, I made continuous checks against the Plasticine model or the drawing using dividers to ensure the proportions were correct. I also marked guidelines to ensure cuts were made in the correct place.

After this initial rounding, the model started to resemble a bird. At this stage, I drew a line to mark the edges of the wings both where they met the underside and also where they divided on the back. Then I followed along these pencil lines using a 6mm, ¼in gouge as a first pass to accentuate the wings.

Using the rotary rasp, I flattened the two planes of the wings so the cross section resembled those in the drawing. I followed this by refining the shape of the breast, the underside around the legs, and the area under the

tail, and I blocked out and rounded the shape of the base the bird stood on.

When the general shape of the base was correct, I blocked in the shape of the feet and legs but avoided any detail at this stage.

The next part to be developed was the head and neck which I carefully refined while making constant checks to ensure not too much wood was being removed.

I accentuated and deepened the area between the tips of the wings on the bird's back and drew in the line that marked the boundary between the back and tail feathers.

I then cut down the sides of the tail and the tips of the wings with a coping saw and removed the small wedge-shaped pieces of waste in these areas.

I had now made at least one pass over the complete carving to develop the shape.

The technique I like to use is an iterative process whereby the overall shape is gradually refined and not finished in any one part. To this end I worked the complete shape a little at a time with the amount of wood being removed getting progressively less.

I also spent more time looking and judging the shape than actually cutting, because an over enthusiastic cut could ruin the piece.

After two or three sessions gradually improving the shape, it was time to start carving some detail. A scalpel proved excellent for the very delicate areas, such as the beak and tail.

Making very small cuts, the beak and the areas where the beak joined the head were carved to the finished size.

To create the individual toes from the blocked in feet, I used a parting tool and a small cutter in a mini drill

Top left **Blocking in the feet and legs.**
Above **After the first complete pass.**
Centre left **Using a scalpel for fine detail.**
Below left **Riffling between the toes.**
Right **Stages in carving the feet and legs.**

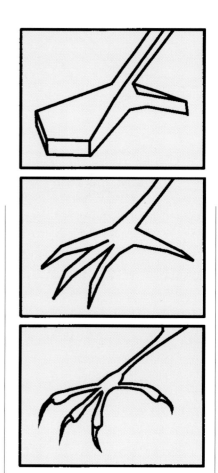

and then smoothed with a riffler, which was the tool of choice for smoothing other areas of the body prior to final finishing.

The mini drill with an appropriate cutter was also a useful tool for getting into the areas other tools could not reach. For example, the under parts at the back of the legs and the sides of the tail where it met the wings.

The tail was thinned and shaped using a scalpel, and various files and rifflers were used to smooth it. The shape of the wings was given a final trim and some feather details were carved into them using a 12mm, ½in gouge to get the correct radius of the feather edges.

The technique was to cut around the curved shape of the feathers using a gouge with approximately the same radius as the feather edges, and using a downwards push or stabbing cut.

Then, holding the chisel almost horizontally, the waste up to the first cuts was sliced away, to get a ledge effect which would accentuate the edge of the feathers.

Next the eyes were carved using the same technique as for carving the feathers.

The carving now looked fairly complete but required a smooth finish.

I used small folded pieces of medium grade glass paper for the bird and put a tooled finish on the base with a small gouge.

As the shape became smoother it accentuated any errors, such as unwanted local bumps and hollows, which were easily put in with a rotary

file. So in practice you might have to abandon smoothing with the glass paper and rework the shapes a little several times during the finishing process.

FINISHING

I sought to achieve a smooth shape with a satin finish showing the depth and colour of the grain. After the fine glass paper, I used a piece of extra fine wet and dry silicon-carbide paper to get a flaw-free, ultra smooth surface.

I do not use satin varnish for every coat when I want to get a good satin finish on a carving, only the last one. This is because nearly all clear satin varnish is gloss varnish with small particles suspended in it to deflect the light and give a satin effect, as opposed to the high shine achieved with gloss.

So if three or four satin coats are applied, the suspended particles might start to obscure or dull the wood grain.

Put on two or three coats of gloss varnish to build up and fill in the pores and get a smooth surface, before giving it a gentle rub down with kitchen scouring powder and putting on the final coat of satin finish.

In this way the required satin surface is achieved and the colour and figure of the wood is not dulled. ●

GIVE HIM A HAND

PROJECT

DEREK OLDBURY SHOWS HOW HE CARVED A PAIR OF HANDS AS A THANK YOU TO THE SURGEON WHO SAVED HIS HANDS

When I first considered this project the object was a simple one, to carve a pair of hands, palms upwards.

I had only to select a suitable piece of wood, decide on a design, and start carving.

But I soon realised this project had several aspects, of which carving was only the obvious one.

There was also a story to tell, technical details to explain, and the progress of the work illustrated by slides taken at suitable stages.

I am a self-employed woodcarver as well as a part-time tutor to Penwith adult education students of woodcarving. It is essential for my hands to be strong, supple and free from pain in order to apply the manual skills needed in carving.

So it was with a sense of fear I realised something was wrong with my hands. At first there were sensations like electric shocks, then an increase in clumsiness and finally some of the knuckle joints began to lock.

A hospital investigation diagnosed carpal tunnel syndrome. The nerves running through a tunnel in the wrist were being choked. The eventual outcome would be loss of control of the hands.

But I was fortunate in having the services of surgeon Tom Scott, an expert in micro surgery, who operated on both hands and restored them to normal.

This project is my tangible expression of thanks to him for restoring the use of my hands, and proof that his skill has restored mine.

WOOD CHOICE

I visited my local wood supplier Cornish Woodcrafts and spoke to Steve Collett about my requirements.

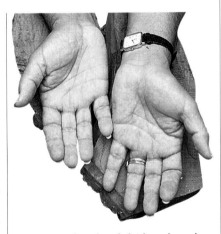

Plan view of my hands laid on the oak block to draw an outline.

He pointed to a clutter of Cornish oak trunk sections, salvaged from Lanhydrock House following storm damage. On the wet ground stood a section of trunk which had been roughly chainsawed.

It leaned sideways, like the Tower of Pisa. This conjured up in my mind a pair of hands stretched upward and outward.

"It's wet and full of shakes and yours for a fiver" said Steve. And so this mature piece of Cornish oak became mine.

Steve cut away excess timber with a bandsaw leaving a shape which was the crude basis of my carving.

I was soon to find problems inherent in the wood and arising from the orientation of the hands. There were physical problems due to the nature and direction of the grain.

First, deep shakes revealed their presence as the wood dried, and the orientation of the hands meant I was forced to carve into end grain, cross and contra grain when establishing the curvature of the fingers and hollowness of the palms.

This required the use of very sharp gouges worked by hand rather than the mallet.

I used an electric drill to produce small areas peppered with drill holes where fragmented wood could easily be removed with least risk to the precious cutting edges of my gouges.

I eliminated several of the shakes which appeared by incorporating them into the spaces between fingers. Others I filled with a mixture of oaken slivers and heavy duty Araldite, pinching them closed with small clamps.

Most of the shakes were radials emanating from the trunk centre and splitting open as the wood dried.

Fortunately I was able to position the fingers so as to avoid most of them.

METHOD

The initial shape of the oak block was of a leaning cube. The intended design consisted of both forearms inclined from a simple integral base, with slightly cupped hands facing upwards and close together. I hoped the hands would balance firmly without tipping over.

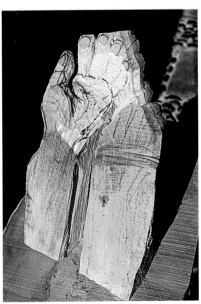

The initial carving of the left hand. The thumb is isolated from the fingers and the palm hollowed.

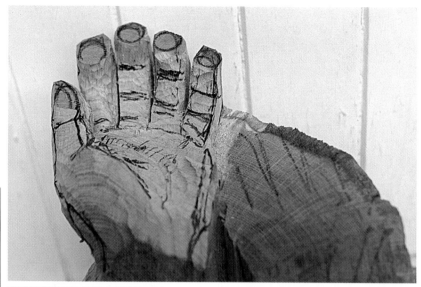

Top left **Fingers are separated and curved. The inner surface of the ring finger has developed a shake.**
Top right **An electric drill helps remove excess hard wood from the back of the hand.**
Below left **A shake eventually splits the ring finger along its length.**
Below right **Fine carving of the left hand continues and rough carving of the right hand begins.**

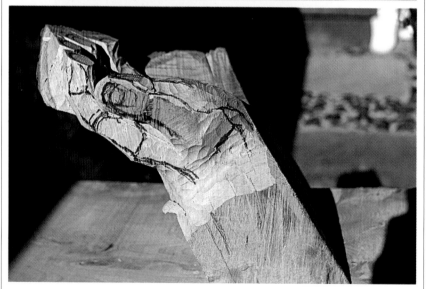

Top **Hollowing of the palm is increased, the fingers separated by saw cuts and the knuckles marked out.**
Centre **Front view showing separation of the fingers with narrow saw cuts.**
Above **Excess wood is removed from the back of the hand.**

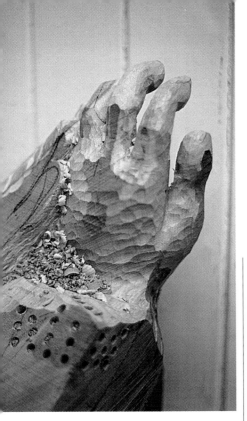

The work piece was firmly gripped by the jaws of a Tiranti chops and I removed the greater amount of unwanted wood using a combination of electric drill and medium/heavy gouges.

I began carving the left hand and established the spaces between the fingers using a coping saw, and carefully carved the shapes of the fingers using lightweight fish tailed gouges.

In the act of cutting I exerted a

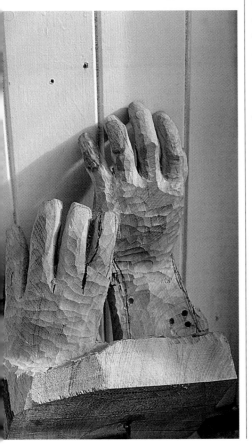

Top **Deep seated shakes in the ring finger of the left hand and middle finger of the right hand.**
Above **Shakes repaired and fine carving of both hands completed.**
Above right **Hands, finished and wax polished.**

....

longitudinal push to the gouge and at the same time imparted a lateral sliding action so the resulting cut had a slicing motion. This was necessary to avoid cracking the relatively thin fingers.

I hollowed out the palm at the same time as refining the fingers to keep the hand as a single element. The right hand was carved in the same way.

I rubbed down the surfaces using fine grit paper and applied two coats of teak oil which brought out the translucency of the surface. I then gave them a final coating of beeswax. The finished surface was translucent, glossy and silky to the touch.

Finally at the finish of his morning surgery in Hayle I was able to 'hand over' my carving to Surgeon Tom Scott, and express my thanks in the most personal and practical way. ●

Cornish Woodcrafts, Rose Cottage, Shortcross Road, Mount Hawke, Nr Truro, Cornwall TR4 8DU. Tel: 01209 890277.

Alec Tiranti Ltd, 70 High Street, Theale, Reading RG7 5AR. Tel: 0118 930 2775.

Derek Oldbury was an engineer and scientist as well as lecturer at Luton University for 24 years before he took early retirement and moved to St Ives, Cornwall nine years ago.
He took up carving about 20 years ago as an antidote to academic work and now teaches adult education classes in carving. He also has space in the local craft market where he takes commissions.

CARVE A PLAYFUL KITTEN

JEREMY WILLIAMS DESCRIBES HOW HE WENT ABOUT CARVING A LIFE-SIZE KITTEN INCORPORATING AS MUCH FEELING OF MOVEMENT AND PLAYFUL ACTION AS POSSIBLE

Completed carving.

In describing this project I have added what I hope will be useful suggestions and advice for anyone who has recently taken up carving as a hobby. Treat yourself! Go for a really good and attractive piece of wood like walnut (*Juglans regia*).

The block I used measured 120mm, 4¾in square and a little over 305mm, 12in long. Walnut is not cheap to buy. My piece cost just under £20 but I think it is worth every penny.

Walnut has qualities possessed by few other woods. It is close grained, yet is seldom too difficult to work by hand, and it takes detail well, even though the figuring may be wild. Walnut can also have beautiful chromatic variations in hue.

If you do buy expensive timber, use it. Don't hoard it away, thinking because it cost a fair bit of money you should keep it for when you do something really good.

I have fallen into that trap more than once. Guess what happens, you hide it away and when, years later, you

get around to using it you find the woodworm have got there first!

PROFILE VIEW

Drawing 1 shows the profile I used. Note the full extent of the tail is not shown as it is curved to follow the grain within the block, which will be seen in the photographs.

The main point is to capture the feeling of alertness and movement, and to do that it is essential to keep your options open as long as possible in areas like the legs and paws, so adjustments can be made as you go along.

For example, I started with the legs shown by the dotted lines. Later I needed to cut them back to where the unbroken lines are drawn to give a better playful look, and at the same time to allow more access to the face.

Changes were also made to the disposition of the ears. They started off

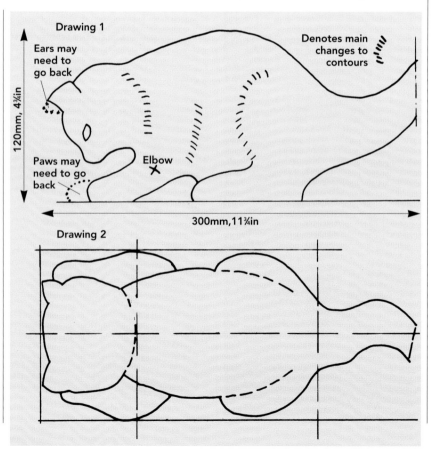

Drawing 1

Ears may need to go back

120mm, 4¾in

Paws may need to go back

Elbow ✗

Denotes main changes to contours

300mm, 11¾in

Drawing 2

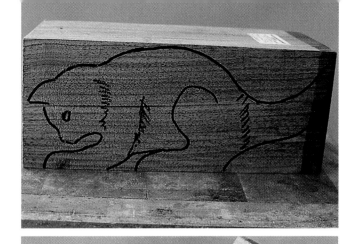

well forward, but were trimmed back once the carving got under way.

Allowing for such changes does mean that when the drawing is applied to the wood, with carbon paper in the usual manner, profile features can look a little out of proportion, but this is intentional.

Nothing is worse than finding yourself boxed in by having cut the dimensions too tight. It can be a real comfort to know you have wood to spare.

PLAN VIEW

Essentially, the design uses flowing lines to impart the sense of movement, and to complement the pronounced figuring of the walnut. In itself the shape is not complex, and to a great degree it is best to feel your way as much as you can where the plan view is concerned.

In other words be guided by the natural composition of the timber and not by the dictates of a strictly drawn plan.

Of course, some initial sketching, even cat-watching, will be needed to ensure you get proportions right to capture the effect of a kitten at play.

Drawing 2 is intended as a guide. The salient points to note are:

1, The ratio of head to body. Do not make the head too small. Keeping it larger than life will help to avoid the pea-on-a-drum syndrome. You can always reduce the size later if you wish.

2, Make certain you have plenty of material to develop the forelegs at the elbows. In a pouncing position the kitten would not hold its forelegs close to its body. The elbows would turn outwards from the sides, just as we tend to do when we thrust our arms and hands up in front of our face.

3, Do not slim down the hindquarters. After the width of the elbows, these are the widest part of the body.

INITIAL CUTTING

The profile outline was cut using a bandsaw. If you don't have one, use a series of saw cuts to notch the wood, making sure you do not saw completely

Top and right
Cutting around the profile drawing applied to the wood. Go with the flow of the grain for the tail.

....

up to the design line. Then chop out as much of the waste as you can. With this method it is preferable to have the profile drawn on both sides of the block.

If you use thin paper like layout paper and draw the design with a felt tip pen, it is a simple matter to reverse the image to give the second side imprint, but remember careful alignment will be needed. This second imprint, though, is not necessary if a bandsaw is to be used.

Do be aware right from the outset that there is not much space between the lower jaw and the forelegs. As the shape of the legs is carved there will be more access created, but you do need to be careful not to undercut the jaw line, nor to make the neck too slim.

If you are planning to use a workholder that necessitates screw fixing the carving wood, keep some of the sawdust from the cutting to fill the screw holes.

When the profile has been cut to shape, it is tempting to draw the plan view on the wood and immediately cut off any surplus material. Don't!

You will have lost all or most of any safety margin you might have needed to execute a fully rounded body without any flat spots. True three-dimensional work demands the fullest use be made of body contours. This means having plenty of wood in hand to start with.

When you see carvings with flat, not rounded, sides it is a fair clue there

was little or no wood spare when the initial roughing out was done.

Rather than bandsawing off all the surplus wood of the plan view in one go, which could have locked me into an awkward situation, I just cut the area on either side of the forelegs and around the tail. The remaining features were delineated as I carved.

ROUGHING OUT

I progressed slowly with the roughing out, not staying too long in any one spot for fear of allowing the work to become unbalanced. Every time the centre line was cut away or any detail was obliterated, it was immediately put back in.

Not all the work was carried out with gouges. Some minor surgery was done with a small saw, like nibbling away around the head.

At this stage I fixed the length I would use for the forelegs, judging what looked right by eye rather than by measurement. Those readers new to carving may be encouraged by the old maxim "If it looks right, it is right".

As you work, be aware how the overall shape develops. Look at it from all angles, not just from the side view. Use your sense of touch, as stroking the wood will detect excess humps.

PROGRESSION

I started by producing a rounded shape either side of the centre of the back. To

From top to bottom

- Cut edges inwards to prevent splitting.
- For end-grain cutting use a small, well-sharpened gouge or chisel.
- A No 3 fishtail is a good tool for shaping the outside curves of the ears ...
- ... and the hollows can be made with a spoon.
- Use an inverted gouge to round the forelegs.

do this I used a 12mm, ½in No 9 gouge to quickly remove waste wood. I aimed to take chips around 3mm, ⅛in in thickness. I left sufficient wood for the hindquarter flanks.

For the less steeply curved parts I preferred to work with a 12mm, ½in No 7 tool, refining the cuts with a No 5.

As soon as I could I outlined the approximate shape of the ears by stab-cutting. Then I shaped the head.

Symmetry of form is best accomplished by making a few cuts on one side then immediately repeating the same cuts on the other side. It is as if the brain recognises the mirror image more easily.

To stop the wood splitting on any edge I always worked the cuts back towards the wood, not away from the edge. This meant the stress on the wood being cut was supported by neighbouring timber.

VISUALISATION

The more you can mentally see the shapes the better. Constant referral to illustrations can be something of a drawback. Not only do other people's drawings, or paintings for that matter, invariably contain elements of artistic licence, which may be prone to amplification when copied, but there can be technical problems when translating a picture to a carving.

Problems such as foreshortened perspective, or parallax, which while acceptable in two-dimensional work are certainly not needed in three-dimensional sculpture.

There is also the point that individuality of expression can only be fully achieved if the work is totally a product of your own mind, but this is something that comes with practice. Initially all of us have to start by referring to published work, or to photographs we have taken.

In the case of the kitten, much of the visualisation related to the animal's basic anatomy. For instance, I spent

time concentrating on the formation of the leg muscles, to give the impression of pent-up power, and the inclusion of a slight depression between the shoulder blades to improve tactile quality.

HEAD

Once the body contours had been roughed out, I concentrated on forming the shape of the head. I preferred to do it this way, as imbalance could have occurred if the body was fully completed before the head was started.

Points to watch are:

1, Do not widen the gap between the ears too soon. You need to establish the final width of the head first.

2, Remember the head is very much like the shape of a ball. Keep it spherical. So often heads are carved far too flat. There should be a distinct curve to the brow across its width, as well as up from the bridge of the nose.

3, Make the eyes reasonably large.

4, Do not make the ears too weak.

As the brow was mainly on end-grain I preferred to use small and very sharp gouges such as a 6mm, ¼in No 5, or Swiss No 7, and to finish with a small chisel where necessary.

While some rasp work may be needed to get the shape you want there is bound to be severe distress to the cell ends of the grain if done to excess, and this could make the finish patchy when polished.

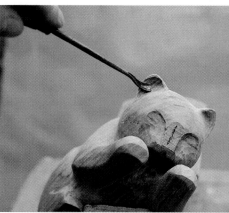

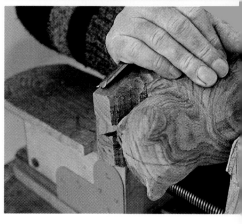

From top to bottom
● Using a No 9, quick cut gouge to shape the underside. Carver's chops are useful as they do not crush the wood.
● Aim for plenty of twist to the tail. Use centre lines on either side and top and bottom.
● Shape using a round Surform.
● Stab cut the shape of the eyes.
● Using a goose neck scraper.

EARS

Note the ears are not at the widest point of the skull. They lie where the head narrows in width before it rises up to the crown.

Shaping the ears is a two-fold operation. For the convex shape of the outside I used a 19mm, ¾in fishtail No 3. The shape of the fishtail affords good visibility. It is necessary to make sure the bottom of each ear blends nicely into the head with a small radius-type cut made with a small half round gouge, or veiner.

Avoid forming the ears so they look as if they have been stuck on. The inside hollows were made with a small No 29 spoon, using a rotational cutting action in preference to using a burr.

FEET AND LEGS

Remember seeing animals' footprints in the snow? Then you will know the feet are placed under the body, with the hind feet a little wider apart than the front ones. They are not outside the body like a pantomime horse!

I am sure you will at some time have noticed how the front legs change direction at their midway elbow joints, so the legs fall under the body when the animal is standing or walking. The same applies to the springing pose.

As mentioned earlier, in this carving's pose the front legs stick out at the elbows. The hind legs are tucked under the body, with only the hocks visible from behind.

Some of the round, sectional shape of the forelegs can be carried out using the blade of a fairly flat gouge, a No 4 for example, upside down.

This is a typical instance when the tool benefits from having a small bevel on the inside edge of the blade. The inside of the legs and the breast of the body can be cut with back bent spoons or shaped with coarse grade abrasive cloth.

I gave the fronts of the feet a slight lift, which again engenders a feeling of motion. It helps to turn the carving over to do this work, as it does when cutting waste between the forelegs themselves with a 6mm, ¼in No 9 gouge. The 12mm, ½in version is also useful for separating hind and forelegs.

One of the advantages of using carver's chops is the jaws are cushioned to prevent the wood from being crushed. With an ordinary woodwork vice, cushioning can be provided with carpet underlay or kitchen sponges.

REFINING THE SHAPE

It is possible to rasp all over the carving to eradicate deep tool cuts, but it takes time and is not much fun. It is better to refine the shape using shallow cutting tools, like 7s, 5s, 4s and 3s. Rasps and Surforms are ideal shaping tools for the tail.

To check where there is extra wood to be removed, use your fingers and thumbs. You will feel the difference better than seeing it.

Adult cats have tails with little or no taper, but kittens' tails tend to run to a point. Neither are totally round in section, being flatter on their upper and lower surfaces than on the sides.

I aimed to give the tail plenty of twist, to impart movement. Blend the base of the tail into the body with gentle curves at the junction. When shaping, I used centre lines on all four sides and plotted the curve in sympathy with the run of the grain.

It is essential to keep it good and thick, otherwise it can end up looking like a rat's tail. A Surform type rasp, or a regular wood rasp is a safe way of getting the concave shaping done. Only a small amount of wood is taken off with every stroke, and this means you have plenty of time to check on your progress.

For the outer (convex) curves, a spokeshave works well. Many, though, will prefer to stick to using a rasp, or even coarse sanding paper.

EYES, NOSE AND MOUTH

Throughout the carving of the eyes and nose, it is essential to use a centre line

Left **Sanding sticks help to even out the pressure.**
Below left **Completed carving,**

and to be sure to always bisect it at right angles when plotting detail.

Blend the nose to the face with the radius of a small No 11 veiner. This gives a softer looking line. Shape the nostrils with a small No 5 for greater emphasis.

Set in the eyes at least one width apart, a little more if possible, and use parallel lines drawn to ensure they are level. Remember, the eyes of a kitten are proportionally larger looking than an adult cat. I outlined their shape with stab cuts, but did not cut too deeply in case I needed to make changes later.

Using callipers I checked the eyes were the same size. It is easy to overlook this and to end up with eyes of a different size.

Whether the eyes are fully open and round or somewhat elliptical in shape, is a personal choice. It may even depend on the tools you have. Aim to get the curves of the lids the same on each eye. Allow the gouges' sweeps to do this for you or you just might end up with a blinking cat!

The eyeballs have to be rounded using a small knife or a tiny chisel. You can cut in a slit for the pupils, or do as I did and shape the eyeballs with a lateral ridge across their widest part to give a highlight of reflection. Clean up with a folded triangle of sanding paper.

In this pose there is no real need to show the mouth, as it is tucked well under. The division of the lips can be carved with a sharp V-tool, if there is access, or stab cut with a suitably shaped gouge.

FINISH

At about this stage of a carving I tend to firm up my ideas on the type of finish I shall use. Sometimes it is best to keep an open mind until a fairly late stage, then again those first impressions are often the best.

By this time most of the figuring and colour of the grain will have been revealed, and any blandness will be apparent. Of course, with such a beautiful wood as walnut there should be little doubt that a smooth finish will be more revealing than a tooled one.

There are many times when opting for a tooled finish can be preferable. If nothing else it proves the work has been hand-carved, or at least hand finished. When a lot of rasping has been carried out, which may possibly have torn the wood, a cut surface is going to give a good finish far quicker than a smooth one.

With a smooth finish each and every blemish will need to be eradicated by careful preparation. At the end of the day it has to be a matter of personal choice, for there is neither a right nor a wrong approach.

TIDYING UP

Do not rush to finish. It is tempting to press ahead regardless, but it is wise to take your time. Finish as much as you possibly can with cutting tools before you start using abrasive cloth and papers.

It is a good idea to leave the work for a day or so, then when you pick it up again and have a fresh look you may see things you missed. But do try and avoid embarking on major alterations at this stage. The chances are there will not be much spare wood left for structural changes.

I always tend to work in the traditional way, scraping before sanding, and then thorough sanding prior to applying the polish. The finish sheen should lie within the surface of the wood, not on top of it.

While the regular rectangular cabinet scraper is a great help for flat, or even for shallow convex shapes, the curved goose-neck type is more versatile, allowing you to work it into contours and hollows.

Sanding can be a painstaking business and even after careful work I usually find one or two spots requiring further attention, no matter how hard I try to get each and every blemish eradicated at each sanding grit stage.

I started with 240 grit and followed this with 320, then a 500 grade abrasive. Working in natural light helps to detect blemishes by the shadows cast. Using small pieces of bamboo cane, covered with leather, to wrap the sanding paper or cloth around allows you to work confined areas.

Brown woods seem to respond well to having an oil finish. Light coloured woods are best sealed with shellac or maybe acrylic. The kitten was treated with three coats of Rustin's Danish Oil, allowing plenty of drying time between successive coats, and with each one rubbed back with fine wire wool.

A point to note is if wax is applied too soon after oiling you can get a bluish bloom on the wood. So, the final coat was allowed three days to dry fully, as well as to mature.

Good furniture wax was buffed with a Webrax pad to work it well into the wood, and then buffed once more with a soft cloth. A few days later a further coat of wax was applied. ●

Rustin's Ltd, Drayton Works, Waterloo Rd, London NW2 7TX. Tel: 0181 450 4666.
Webrax is available from:
CSM Trade Supplies, 95-6, Lewes Road, Brighton, East Sussex BN2 3QA. Tel: 01273 600434.

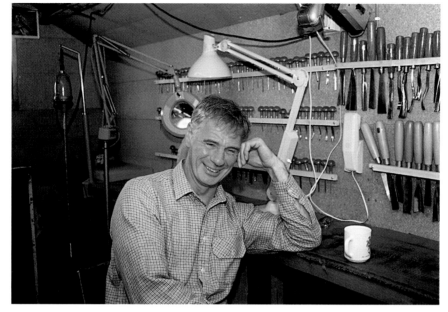

Judith Nicoll meets former coal-miner turned expressionist bird carver, Colin Hickman

JUST HAPPY HERE CARVING

A familiar face to all those who visit woodworking shows across the UK, Colin Hickman is often to be found demonstrating his techniques on the Ashley Iles stand. He still manages to beam with genuine pleasure at each person who enquires "How do you do that?"

His enthusiasm for wildlife and carving is only exceeded by his enjoyment in meeting people and sharing his skills. His style is quite distinctive and

his skills self-taught. He mainly carves birds because he loves them and because he loves carving.

"I've got pictures in my head that are 50 years old. I've seen birds for 50 years and I've really looked at them. I can see how they are because I've studied them all my life."

Top **Colin Hickman in his workshop with some of his tools.**
Above **Heads in various stages of carving, a guide for students.**
Below **Colin's finished bird's head walking sticks.**

Here is a total individual who follows his own principles, and he carves solely what he wishes to with no thought of selling. He will carve an eagle because that is just what he wants to do at that moment.

"I've been pestered to sell things, but I'm not bothered about money, never wanted money. I'm just happy here carving, that's me."

His compositions are personal, individual statements. They are detailed carvings but they are not correct models. He is not one of those influenced by pattern books, photographs or paintings.

He carves what he remembers and has never followed anyone else's style of carving. From his first meeting at a carving club he worked differently from the others there.

Not influenced by taught principles of design and shape, he concentrates on the bird as he remembers its form, shape and character and then he forms it freely with his own style of 'feathering-up.'

He knows his own subject intimately and has a visual memory. The carvings have a vitality and freshness so many of the lifelike models carved by wildlife carving practitioners never achieve. This could be a result of rarely referring to reference material. He has the art of conveying his experience in wildlife, and he sees it as a gift.

Mining

Colin is an ex-collier who has worked as a joiner for the social services since his redundancy.

"Coming out of pits and doing this job is like being on holiday." He admits that when he left school he should have been a joiner and not a collier. "I were forced into it. It were the natural thing for everybody round here to go in the pit. Your dad worked in pit. You worked in pit.

"But I had two bad accidents that forced me out. I

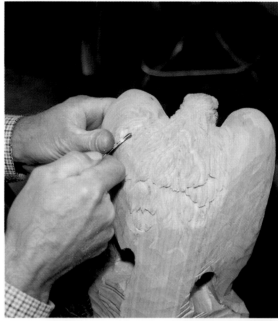

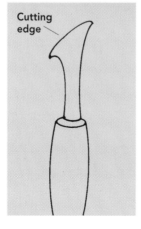

Cutting edge

Top **The ¹⁄₁₆in V-tool is Colin's ideal tool.**
Centre **At work on a carving.**
Left **Colin's carving knife shape.**

had a pony run over me with two tubs of mortar on. That broke a lot of bones, and then I had disc problems. But it don't affect my carving at all. I can sit and carve 24 hours a day. Miners are very strong in the arms and shoulders because they've been digging 20 tons of coal a day."

His father unwittingly instilled in him more than just the pit. He had the colliers' love of birds. Canaries were introduced to pits in the 18th century when it was discovered they reacted to much lower levels of carbon monoxide than humans. Since 1956 it has been law for every coal mine to keep at least one pair, as they saved lives.

Pit managers and colliers used to take care of them in the mine like family pets. Colin's father kept British finches and linnets at home and a neighbour in Sutton Ashfield also had a large aviary. From the age of three Colin was out bird-nesting.

"I had best egg collection in Nottinghamshire when I were 13 years old. It's all illegal now."

He started carving about 14 years ago to make a walking stick for his lad. On holiday at a Norfolk auction, they had seen a carved stick with an English setter's head, just like his son's dog. He wanted to buy it but it went for £90, so he vowed to make one instead.

He used a Stanley knife and some Australian jarrah wood (*Eucalyptus marginata*). "Red wood as hard as iron, and I enjoyed every second of it." Colin showed the result to an experienced carver who said, "It's good. But what made you want to carve a camel?"

Colin quickly retorted that he'd always liked camels, and took the offending article home and worked on it until he'd perfected it.

He enjoyed the carving so much he went to a local carving club where the man Colin admires more than any other, Arthur Bracka of Mansfield, was visiting. He set them a task to

Eagles with dinner guest. Colin carves from the feathers in.

carve an owl. He gave them bandsawn owls and showed them his finished one.

At the end Colin's owl was completely different from the other 15, as he had carved feathers into it. He wanted it to look right, not that theirs were wrong, he just wanted it his own way.

"Doing it my way was all right as I could always go back to his way if mine didn't work." How many people have the confidence to begin at the beginning with their own style?

Unused talent

Colin's enthusiasm extends to his demonstrations, and the reason for this is he loves to share what he does. Both of us agree there is a lot of unused talent out there, and because we like what we do, we want others to enjoy it too.

"I want to see more people stop watching telly and make a good carving. I want to promote carving. I think there's a lot of people out there who could carve really fantastic, but they want a bit of encouragement. If I can get one in a hundred to start carving that would be nice, wouldn't it?" We agree that anyone can do it.

He told me a wonderful story of his pit manager putting on an exhibition of colliers' own hobby work during the national strike. The police, who were bussed in from all over the country, were amazed at the varied skills.

"They thought colliers were all cloth caps, whippets and pigeons." One inspector who bought one of Colin's carvings told him, "If all the police forces in the country got together they couldn't put on a show as good as this."

It is often when carvers talk to me about their teaching, they reveal most about their ideas and techniques.

He demonstrates and explains indefatigably at shows, and he teaches in his workshop at home. Often, people with a natural gift find it difficult to explain how they do it. But Colin has a simple approach. Surrounded now by immaculate rows of gleaming tools, he explains that only half a dozen are needed for his free style of carving birds in the round.

His 'desert island, one and only tool' would be the ⅟₁₆in V-tool, and then the number 40 back bent V-tool. He uses a ½in gouge, a ¼in gouge, and a knife which he draws for me. He adds this knife is in production but it is too big for him.

With furniture carving. "...you have to have the tool to fit the pattern," but with his birds he mainly uses the V-tool which "...will carve human hair, hair on dogs and feathers on birds."

He does not shape the bird with large gouges and then detail the feathers. He actually shapes the bird with flowing feathers using the small V-tool as he goes along.

"There's no set pattern. I look at it as a tile on a roof, everything on a bird is designed for the water to come off. Everything flows down."

He demonstrates the use of the V-tool for me but points out that although it is simple you do have to know where the feathers flow.

Sharpening

Before anything the beginner is told a sharpening system is needed. No tool is any good if blunt.

"The priorities are sharpening, then tools and the right timber."

Novices are advised to start simply, with a relief carving. A good start is a children's drawing book with a picture, such as the old woman who lived in a shoe. Every technique is required, for shoe laces, faces, tiles on the roof and so on.

He suggests two or three relief carvings and by then people will understand what they want to do next. "Everyone's got a flair for something, haven't they?"

I ask about the next problem and he answers that once they've got their wood people don't realise they have to draw onto it.

"You have to trace it out for them, then explain where to cut, and then what tool to use. They'll pick a tool they feel comfortable with and is right for them." Later he explains other tools, and people learn to feel comfortable with those.

"I can't stress it enough. If people want to carve, the most important thing about wood carving is having sharp tools." If they want to carve birds, he's their man. "I want other people to do what I'm doing. I want someone to come here and then to go out there far better than me, but I've taught them."

Timber for Colin usually comes from local woods. His walking sticks are hazel (*Corylus avellana*) or rhododendron (*Rhododendron ponticum*) and he looks for a shape without cross grain.

For smooth carvings he recommends lime (*Tilia vulgaris*) as it takes detail and the beauty can be in the detail and not the wood. Imagine the grain of elm (*Ulmus spp.*) across the smooth carving of a face! With a smooth carving you need a nice fruit wood such as damson or cherry (*Prunus spp.*).

Faults in the timber don't bother Colin when they come up during the process, as he just "...blinds it with detail," by feathering it up. As a planner, pattern maker and bandsawer myself, I am fascinated by his approach.

"I don't plan nothing. I just carve it. I've got to let the bird do what it wants to do. I don't use a bandsaw as you're stuck with that shape, full stop. With a lump of wood you can do what you like with it. If you want to put a wing out or change the angle of the tail you can."

Left **Blackbirds.**
Below left **A starling.**
Below **Owl.**

Duds

I ask Colin about mistakes, or whether each carving can be altered as he goes along so he has no throwaways. He laughs and picks up a dud from a shelf, "I'll never do that again!"

He tells me about a pair of eagles that started as a pair of pheasants. He put the block of wood on the bench and thought it would just take two pheasants.

He always starts with the head and tries to get the beak first and that tells him how big the head wants to be. Then he judges the proportions.

"If you look at the eagle's beak and pheasant's beak, apart from the sere at the top, they're the same. I started a pheasant's head, and all I could see was an eagle."

So often I have told pupils you are only as good as your research. Colin aims to achieve a different effect from my measured accuracy. "I've no set plan. I don't get a dozen books. I just sit and do it. So when I have a block of wood, I sit and think I might do a robin, I just start carving."

Again I ask about the problems of teaching, because most carvers I meet are unsure of their ideas. The most common question is how to get started. A pattern is a great confidence booster.

However, Colin thinks the shape is easy and it's the detail people find hard, but what they want to learn is detail. They want to run before they can walk.

He does start with guidelines, such as keeping a centre line and certain ways of making cuts. He has some heads carved in different stages to show them. Then they carve what they want to.

"Carving is creating a shape, and if you can see that shape you can draw it out. The hard part about it is putting on the fine detail." Colin does not plan his shapes, they emerge as he comes downwards with flowing feathers.

"There is a difference between people who know how it is, and people who copy the drawing." He is right. If you look at visual images, paintings or photographs, you may immediately see what a blurred or simple shape in the distance is doing.

A simple line will depict for you a man running, or woman sitting, or horse racing: you do not need the detail. An artist draws that line, he does not plan it with patterns. He, like Colin, knows how it is.

I ask Colin which is his best and favourite carving, but he says quickly that he hasn't done it yet. There are many carvings he is not happy with. "If you're happy with what you do you might as well pack up because you need that challenge. You want to better whatever you've done previously."

The eagles are admired but Colin knows he can do better than that. He considers them and muses that one is all right but the other did not quite achieve what he wanted.

What about the future? His face brightens. He would like to carve a pair of fighting cockerels, "To perfection. But it's getting a piece of timber big enough, that's the problem."

I whisper a name to him, and so maybe next year we may see the cockerels emerging from the block. ●

RIVER RAPTOR

ROGER SCHROEDER SHOWS HOW WILDFOWL CARVER ERNEST MUEHLMATT SCULPTED AN OSPREY PERCHED ON A CHANNEL MARKER

The finished osprey atop J4.

The story behind Ernest Muehlmatt's carved osprey began 20 years ago. Muehlmatt, a renown American wildfowl carver, was boating with his family on the St Lawrence river which is a natural boundary between the USA and Canada.

They were awakened one night by a loud crash. In the morning his children found a red marker drifting in the river. It was a channel marker, labelled J4, apparently knocked from its fixed, navigational position by a passing boat.

Muehlmatt let his children take it home. Once back in Springfield, Pennsylvania, Muehlmatt mounted the 1830 x 180mm, 72 x 7in diameter wood post on an iron base.

For the next 20 years it sat in the yard. Then in 1994 Muehlmatt decided to carve an osprey perched on a red channel marker, incorporating a carved copy of J4 as the bird's pedestal.

His inspiration for the bird came from visits to Florida, where he had seen numerous ospreys sitting atop pilings and channel markers.

Also known as fish hawks, ospreys are common from northern Canada to Mexico. The species, almost eagle in size, was dying off owing to ingested pesticides, but in recent years the birds have been making a comeback.

Muehlmatt chose J4 as the perch because he felt the red colour would complement the bird's natural coloration of white and brown.

Muehlmatt titled his finished composition *Red Right Return*. Red buoys are kept to the right when returning to port, he explains. But the title also symbolises the return of the osprey from near extinction.

TUPELO

Muehlmatt decided from the beginning his would be a sculptural piece carved from a single lump of wood.

The problem was finding a block large enough for both bird and post, as

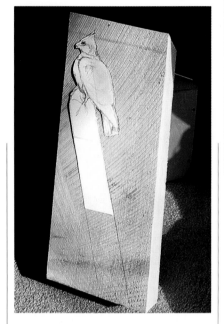

After procuring a sizeable block of tupelo for *Red Right Return*, Muehlmatt laid out the pattern of osprey and post on the wood.

laminating pieces of wood was not what he wanted.

He decided on a massive piece of tupelo (*Nyssa spp*) which he had cut for the composition.

During the 1970s, wildfowl carvers from Louisiana started entering their work at competitions using a wood known by a variety of names: tupelo, white gum, yellow and grey gum, and olive.

The wood grows in a narrow belt about 100 miles wide in the USA. It grows best in swamps, and it can attain heights of 30m, 100ft with diameters of 1,200 to 1,500mm, 48 to 60in.

Tupelo is light in weight, takes great detail, can be worked cross grain, and accepts paints without pitch or resins bleeding through the finish.

But its biggest asset is very thick pieces can be attained and worked without the wood checking.

Muehlmatt called a friend in Louisiana who harvests tupelo straight from the swamps and had him send a piece measuring 1220 x 430 x 355mm, 48 x 17 x 14in.

The supplier said it was the largest piece of wood he had ever cut for a carver. He had to cut down a tree measuring nearly 1525mm, 60in in diameter because the centre of a tupelo tree tends to be too hard to carve.

THE HEAD

Carving began with the head. Muehlmatt felt having a wildfowl head roughed out at the beginning gave him the opportunity to communicate with the bird and vice versa.

To get the head out of the block quickly he used a chainsaw to remove wood from four sides, about 150mm, 6in from the top of the wood, leaving a block on top of a block.

He shaped the features with grinding tools and used callipers to keep the proportions correct. First the beak was carved, then the eyes and last the cheeks.

Muehlmatt used the chainsaw again to give shape to the body. What

Below **A chainsaw took away large slabs of wood from the block, while chainsaw attachments such as the Lancelot did the sculpting.**

Below right **Positioning the bird on the post was important. It was critical not to take too much wood from around the top of the post so the feet could be positioned properly.**

The first step was to bring the head out of the wood, an early reference for the carver. Behind the head is a dust collector.

was on his mind while sawing was where the body would end and the post would begin.

He also had to figure on the position of the feet on the buoy.

"I worked fast but with care not to take too much wood off, especially where the bird joins the marker," he explained.

"Only if I was absolutely sure about taking away wood would I then whack it off." But even with wood being sawn away, the remaining block was unwieldy.

Though he originally wanted a one-piece sculpture, Muehlmatt decided to lighten the block by cutting away part of the post, only to re-attach it later.

The chainsaw could remove chunks of wood but it could not readily follow the contours of hollows and curves of the osprey's body.

LANCELOT

To take away more wood and start to give anatomical definition to the bird, Muehlmatt used an angle grinder and a Lancelot power carving disc. This is actually a chainsaw blade sandwiched between two steel discs, and an angle grinder gives it rotation.

The cutter seems to have little regard for grain direction, hardness of the wood or even knots. It is available in a 22-tooth model for roughing out and a 14-tooth model for a more finished surface.

Muehlmatt used the tool much as he would a scoop to take wood away. He says it was potentially a dangerous tool because of the teeth.

"It's a wood eliminator. It got rid of a tremendous amount of wood. This piece took six weeks from beginning to end, and I could not have done it in that short amount of time without the grinder and Lancelot."

Another grinding tool he found helpful for removing wood was a smaller version of the Lancelot powered by a flexible shaft tool. Though the disc was small, only

The feet, as all parts of the anatomy, were carved from the block of tupelo.

50mm, 2in in diameter, it could cut and remove wood in any direction.

Muehlmatt saw the chainsaw carving accessories as essential for sculpting wood quickly. "They are helpful when you know what wood you want to get rid of," he said. "90 per cent of bird carving is removing excess wood. The rest is just tuning up with feather and other textural details."

Sanding was also done with power tools, nearly all of it using drum sanders fitted in his flexible shaft tool. Fortunately, says Muehlmatt, tupelo sands easily.

CHALLENGES

Some anatomical considerations had to be addressed after nearly all the waste wood had been removed. He wanted one foot of the osprey resting on top of the post, the other foot grasping the side of the marker.

The challenge was having to separate the toe nails of the bird from the wood since he did not want any insertions for the sculpture.

These wind-blown feathers were relieved from the surface using cross-cut cutters and tungsten-carbide roughing and shaping bits.

Giving the head feathers a wind-blown look was another challenge. To raise these feathers he used cross-cut or stump cutters, which had orderly rows of teeth around the bits, and round-shaped tungsten-carbide cutting bits.

For the eyes, Muehlmatt did not go to a taxidermy supply house and purchase them. Instead he made his own using a technique that could be described as fitting a contact lens over painted wood.

He first hand-painted the intricate details of the osprey's eyes on the end of a dowel. He next fashioned a lens made from a sheet of Lucite, which is a clear plastic, and gave it a convex shape using finer and finer sandpaper.

Then he glued the wood to the plastic and cut off a short section of the dowel. He then had an eye which he inserted into the osprey's head.

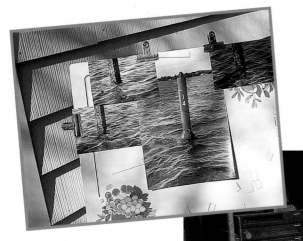

Above **Muehlmatt took photo references of how water flowed around a buoy and wood pilings.**
Right **Muehlmatt built a base to recreate water using 100mm, 4in thick tupelo.**

WATER

The bird and shortened post had lost enough weight so Muehlmatt could re-attach it to the part he had cut away.

At that point, and before he had given the osprey its feather definition, he decided to work on the water the buoy would rest in.

The water base or surface was fashioned from four pieces of 100mm, 4in thick tupelo glued and clamped together. The problem Muehlmatt faced was how to carve the water.

"You think you know what water looks like until you have to carve it," he said with some frustration.

He even went back to Canada to see how J4's replacement (now steel instead of wood) looked in the river. He took photographs of the buoy and other posts in currents.

At first he thought he would have the water flowing around the post. He decided against that, went to work on the base with the carving discs, redid the water twice, and ended up with very gentle waves.

His next crisis was the finish to put on the carved water. At first he thought he would paint the wood to look like water. But he finally painted it a flat black, not blue.

The colour, he felt, would complement the colours of the post and bird while at the same time it would not draw the viewer's eye to it.

PAINT

After sealing the wood, he used a flat black spray paint and rubbed the dried paint with crumpled newsprint. The rubbed effect gave the painted wood a satin sheen.

Muehlmatt also decided the bird and marker were not tall enough, even given the added elevation the water base provided.

To give the bird more height, he added a section of wood between the water base and the post. This addition elevated the sculpture and brought the bird's eyes level with his own.

With the carving of the bird, post and water done, what was left was the fine detailing of the feather groupings.

Above **Much of the water shaping was done with a grinder and the Lancelot power carving disc. The original J4 marker, the model for the sculpture, is in the background.**
Below **Muehlmatt designed a fixture to hold the bird while burning and stoning its surface.**

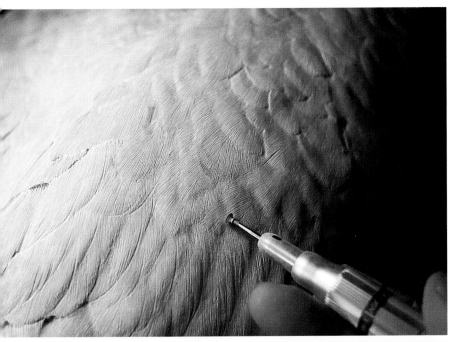

Left **Stoning was done with an inverted cone bit.**
Below left **Muehlmatt did some burning for colour on the bird's face.**

the band, Muehlmatt came up with a piece of birch veneer (*Betula spp*) and painted it to look like metal. All that was left was to paint the post.

Muehlmatt experimented with many shades of red, fearing that too brilliant a red would overpower the bird. Though a typical red navigational marker has to be brightly visible, Muehlmatt toned down the colour with washes of raw umber.

The sculpture stands in Muehlmatt's living room. It is a majestic and dramatic presence among other, smaller wildfowl he has carved or collected.

He hopes some day one of his sons will take it for his own home. Until then it keeps a watchful eye on its maker. ●

Lancelot and Percival power carving tools available in the UK from Craft Supplies Ltd, The Mill, Millers Dale, Nr Buxton, Derbyshire SK17 8SN. Tel: 01298 871636.

Though Muehlmatt often burns areas of his birds to accentuate dark colours, he did a minimum of burning on his osprey. The only areas he burned for colour were the streaking around the eyes and some spots on the chest.

The rest of the feather detail was done using a method called stoning. The stone is actually a bit shaped like an inverted cone and powered by the flexible shaft tool.

Only the edge of the inverted cone cut into the wood, leaving what looked like barb lines.

What helped with detailing such a large bird was a block of wood with a V-groove that supported the sculpture.

Supporting the block was a power arm, a tool that held wood to a base plate. The power arm was designed to allow the wood to be moved at any vertical or horizontal angle.

Muehlmatt estimated nearly half the time spent on the sculpture was devoted to stoning the surface.

FINISHING

With the partial burning and stoning finished, the last step was to paint the osprey and post.

After gessoing the body, Muehlmatt recreated the dark brown colour of the bird using ultramarine blue, burnt umber, and dioxazine purple. To give the bird its white colour he used gesso.

After J4 was dislodged and then salvaged by Muehlmatt's children, it retained a wide galvanised metal band around the post.

Rather than using metal to recreate

Roger Schroeder is a prolific writer and lecturer on woodworking, construction, sculpture and carving, as well as a cabinet-maker and amateur carver. He combines these activities with a full-time job as a high school English teacher, specialising in teaching creative writing and research.

INDEX

TITLES AVAILABLE FROM
GMC Publications

BOOKS

WOODWORKING

40 More Woodworking Plans & Projects . . . . *GMC Publications*
Bird Boxes and Feeders for the Garden . . . . *Dave Mackenzie*
Complete Woodfinishing . . . . *Ian Hosker*
Electric Woodwork . . . . *Jeremy Broun*
Furniture & Cabinetmaking Projects . . . . *GMC Publications*
Furniture Projects . . . . *Rod Wales*
Furniture Restoration (Practical Crafts) . . . . *Kevin Jan Bonner*
Furniture Restoration and Repair for Beginners . . . . . . *Kevin Jan Bonner*
Green Woodwork . . . . *Mike Abbott*
The Incredible Router . . . . *Jeremy Broun*
Making & Modifying Woodworking Tools . . . . *Jim Kingshott*
Making Chairs and Tables . . . . *GMC Publications*
Making Fine Furniture . . . . *Tom Darby*
Making Little Boxes from Wood . . . . *John Bennett*
Making Shaker Furniture . . . . *Barry Jackson*
Pine Furniture Projects for the Home . . . . *Dave Mackenzie*
Sharpening Pocket Reference Book . . . . *Jim Kingshott*
Sharpening: The Complete Guide . . . . *Jim Kingshott*
Stickmaking: A Complete Course . . . . *Andrew Jones & Clive George*
Woodfinishing Handbook (Practical Crafts) . . . . *Ian Hosker*
Woodworking Plans and Projects . . . . *GMC Publications*
The Workshop . . . . *Jim Kingshott*

WOODTURNING

Adventures in Woodturning . . . . *David Springett*
Bert Marsh: Woodturner . . . . *Bert Marsh*
Bill Jones' Notes from the Turning Shop . . . . *Bill Jones*
Bill Jones' Further Notes from the Turning Shop . . . . *Bill Jones*
Colouring Techniques for Woodturners . . . . *Jan Sanders*
Decorative Techniques for Woodturners . . . . *Hilary Bowen*
Essential Tips for Woodturners . . . . *GMC Publications*
Faceplate Turning . . . . *GMC Publications*
Fun at the Lathe . . . . *R.C. Bell*
Illustrated Woodturning Techniques . . . . *John Hunnex*
Intermediate Woodturning Projects . . . . *GMC Publications*
Keith Rowley's Woodturning Projects . . . . *Keith Rowley*
Make Money from Woodturning . . . . *Ann & Bob Phillips*
Multi-Centre Woodturning . . . . *Ray Hopper*
Pleasure and Profit from Woodturning . . . . *Reg Sherwin*
Practical Tips for Turners & Carvers . . . . *GMC Publications*
Practical Tips for Woodturners . . . . *GMC Publications*
Spindle Turning . . . . *GMC Publications*
Turning Miniatures in Wood . . . . *John Sainsbury*
Turning Wooden Toys . . . . *Terry Lawrence*

Understanding Woodturning . . . . *Ann & Bob Phillips*
Useful Techniques for Woodturners . . . . *GMC Publications*
Useful Woodturning Projects . . . . *GMC Publications*
Woodturning: A Foundation Course . . . . *Keith Rowley*
Woodturning: A Source Book of Shapes . . . . *John Hunnex*
Woodturning Jewellery . . . . *Hilary Bowen*
Woodturning Masterclass . . . . *Tony Boase*
Woodturning Techniques . . . . *GMC Publications*
Woodturning Test Reports . . . . *GMC Publications*
Woodturning Wizardry . . . . *David Springett*

WOODCARVING

The Art of the Woodcarver . . . . *GMC Publications*
Carving Birds & Beasts . . . . *GMC Publications*
Carving on Turning . . . . *Chris Pye*
Carving Realistic Birds . . . . *David Tippey*
Decorative Woodcarving . . . . *Jeremy Williams*
Essential Tips for Woodcarvers . . . . *GMC Publications*
Essential Woodcarving Techniques . . . . *Dick Onians*
Lettercarving in Wood: A Practical Course . . . . *Chris Pye*
Practical Tips for Turners & Carvers . . . . *GMC Publications*
Understanding Woodcarving . . . . *GMC Publications*
Useful Techniques for Woodcarvers . . . . *GMC Publications*
Wildfowl Carving - Volume 1 . . . . *Jim Pearce*
Wildfowl Carving - Volume 2 . . . . *Jim Pearce*
The Woodcarvers . . . . *GMC Publications*
Woodcarving: A Complete Course . . . . *Ron Butterfield*
Woodcarving: A Foundation Course . . . . *Zoë Gertner*
Woodcarving for Beginners . . . . *GMC Publications*
Woodcarving Test Reports . . . . *GMC Publications*
Woodcarving Tools, Materials & Equipment . . . . *Chris Pye*

UPHOLSTERY

Seat Weaving (Practical Crafts) . . . . *Ricky Holdstock*
Upholsterer's Pocket Reference Book . . . . *David James*
Upholstery: A Complete Course . . . . *David James*
Upholstery Restoration . . . . *David James*
Upholstery Techniques & Projects . . . . *David James*

TOYMAKING

Designing & Making Wooden Toys . . . . *Terry Kelly*
Fun to Make Wooden Toys & Games . . . . *Jeff & Jennie Loader*
Making Board, Peg & Dice Games . . . . *Jeff & Jennie Loader*
Making Wooden Toys & Games . . . . *Jeff & Jennie Loader*
Restoring Rocking Horses . . . . *Clive Green & Anthony Dew*

DOLLS' HOUSES

Architecture for Dolls' Houses . . . . *Joyce Percival*
Beginners' Guide to the Dolls' House Hobby . . . . *Jean Nisbett*
The Complete Dolls' House Book . . . . *Jean Nisbett*
Dolls' House Bathrooms: Lots of Little Loos . . . . *Patricia King*
Easy to Make Dolls' House Accessories . . . . *Andrea Barham*
Make Your Own Dolls' House Furniture . . . . *Maurice Harper*
Making Dolls' House Furniture . . . . *Patricia King*
Making Georgian Dolls' Houses . . . . *Derek Rowbottom*
Making Miniature Oriental Rugs & Carpets . . . *Meik & Ian McNaughton*
Making Period Dolls' House Accessories . . . . *Andrea Barham*
Making Period Dolls' House Furniture . . . . . . *Derek & Sheila Rowbottom*
Making Tudor Dolls' Houses . . . . *Derek Rowbottom*
Making Unusual Miniatures . . . . *Graham Spalding*
Making Victorian Dolls' House Furniture . . . . *Patricia King*
Miniature Needlepoint Carpets . . . . *Janet Granger*
The Secrets of the Dolls' House Makers . . . . *Jean Nisbett*

CRAFTS

Celtic Knotwork Designs . . . . *Sheila Sturrock*
Collage from Seeds, Leaves and Flowers . . . . *Joan Carver*
Complete Pyrography . . . . *Stephen Poole*
Creating Knitwear Designs . . . . *Pat Ashforth & Steve Plummer*
Cross Stitch Kitchen Projects . . . . *Janet Granger*
Cross Stitch on Colour . . . . *Sheena Rogers*
Embroidery Tips & Hints . . . . *Harold Hayes*
An Introduction to Crewel Embroidery . . . . *Mave Glenny*
Making Character Bears . . . . *Valerie Tyler*
Making Greetings Cards for Beginners . . . . *Pat Sutherland*
Making Knitwear Fit . . . . *Pat Ashforth & Steve Plummer*
Needlepoint: A Foundation Course . . . . *Sandra Hardy*
Pyrography Handbook (Practical Crafts) . . . . *Stephen Poole*
Tassel Making for Beginners . . . . *Enid Taylor*
Tatting Collage . . . . *Lindsay Rogers*
Temari: A Traditional Japanese Embroidery Technique . *Margaret Ludlow*

THE HOME

Home Ownership: Buying and Maintaining . . . . *Nicholas Snelling*

Security for the Householder:
Fitting Locks and Other Devices . . . . *E.Phillips*

VIDEOS

Drop-in and Pinstuffed Seats . . . . *David James*
Stuffover Upholstery . . . . *David James*
Elliptical Turning . . . . *David Springett*
Woodturning Wizardry . . . . *David Springett*
Turning Between Centres: The Basics . . . . *Dennis White*
Turning Bowls . . . . *Dennis White*
Boxes, Goblets and Screw Threads . . . . *Dennis White*
Novelties and Projects . . . . *Dennis White*
Classic Profiles . . . . *Dennis White*

Twists and Advanced Turning . . . . *Dennis White*
Sharpening the Professional Way . . . . *Jim Kingshott*
Sharpening Turning & Carving Tools . . . . *Jim Kingshott*
Bowl Turning . . . . *John Jordan*
Hollow Turning . . . . *John Jordan*
Woodturning: A Foundation Course . . . . *Keith Rowley*
Carving a Figure: The Female Form . . . . *Ray Gonzalez*
The Router: A Beginner's Guide . . . . *Alan Goodsell*
The Scroll Saw: A Beginner's Guide . . . . *John Burke*

MAGAZINES

Woodturning • Woodcarving • Toymaking • Furniture & Cabinetmaking

BusinessMatters • Creative Ideas for the Home • The Router

●

The above represents a full list of all titles currently published or scheduled to be published. All are
available direct from the Publishers or through bookshops, newsagents and specialist retailers. To place an order, or to obtain a
complete catalogue, contact:

GMC Publications,
166 High Street, Lewes, East Sussex BN7 1XU, United Kingdom
Tel: 01273 488005 Fax: 01273 478606

Orders by credit card are accepted